Joyful
Rigor

2nd Edition

Enriching the Intellectual and Spiritual
Lives of Our Children with a Classical
Charlotte Mason Approach

by

KAREN J. RISTUCCIA

THE WILBERFORCE SCHOOL PRESS

Joyful Rigor: Enriching the Intellectual and Spiritual Lives
of Our Children with a Classical Charlotte Mason Approach
2nd Edition 2021

The Wilberforce School Press, P.O. Box 1132, Princeton, NJ 08542

The Wilberforce School Press
P.O. Box 1132
Princeton, NJ 08542
www.wilberforceschool.org

Cover Design by Eve Siegel Design
Typesetting by Rainbow Graphics

ISBN: 978-0-9838940-2-5
Printed in the United States of America

Dedication

As in all I do, I thank the Lord Jesus Christ for his gracious love and enabling. I thank Him as well for giving me my best friend and husband, Matthew, and my wonderful sons and daughters-in-love—Joel and Janet, Nathan and Grace—to accompany me on this pilgrimage of joyful rigor.

Contents

Acknowledgments

I undertake this privilege of acknowledging my helpers and inspirers with trepidation. Because it takes a village to make an educational philosopher, there is not room in this venue to mention all those to whom I am indebted. My teachers in graduate school and beyond have helped me to hone my ideas and to combine idealism with pragmatism. Over the years, I have read hundreds of books on education, taxing my book budget and at times the gracious Princeton Public Library staff and its interlibrary loan system. Each of those books and writers now frames part of my perspective on learning and learners. I am indebted also to The Wilberforce School's sister schools that daily seek to unite classical Christian and Charlotte Mason education and to the individuals from those schools who have served as examples, sounding boards, and supportive friends.

Supremely, I am indebted first to Howe and Brenda Whitman and David and Awilda Rowe, two couples who pioneered The Wilberforce School; next, to Sara Capps Furlich, who worked to translate their vision into The Wilberforce School's first year; and again, to Howe Whitman, who since that time has continued expanding and aligning this translation process. Of course, every idea, every metaphor, every practice owes its continuing life to the dedicated teachers of The Wilberforce School, with whom I have learned, worked, and grown. Along with the board of The Wilberforce School, the school's faculty and staff labor to create and sustain an education that is infused with joy and rigor, discovery and scrutiny, grace and truth. Beyond them, of course, it is both the parents of The Wilberforce School's students who entrust to us their children and those students themselves to whom I owe the particular outworking of my pedagogic ideas. Charlotte Mason reiterated and embodied an education that was "for the children's sake"; it is toward this high standard that we at The Wilberforce School strive.

As a teacher of writing, I must acknowledge the numerous editors who, over the last four years, have enabled me not only to enjoin the writing process but also to experience it. Thanks to all of you for honesty, red pens, and hope.

Finally, I thank the people who have been with me in this journey for so many years, particularly my inspirer Nancy, my goad Laura, and above all, my ever-supportive family—Matt, Joel, Janet, Nathan, and Grace. It is my wish that each person who reads this book will find similar loyal compatriots who will both facilitate rigor and wisely season that rigor with joy.

Foreword

When we started The Wilberforce School in 2005, we begged Sara Capps (now Sara Furlich) to come to Princeton to be our first Head of School. She had been Academic Dean at West Dallas Community School, which served as the model for our school. She agreed to come for one year (as long as we could find a place that allowed her dog, Shamgar) to help us launch the school. We are forever grateful to Sarah for her guidance. I was the Board Chair that year, and Dr. Karen Ristuccia served on the founding board.

In any new enterprise, there are a large number of tasks that need to be done, and done well, all at the same time, on day one. It was a very busy time. So, when Sara suggested that we start publishing *The Wilberforce Weekly*, the first week of school, I balked. We had our hands full with other essential tasks. There was no time to add a weekly publication. But somehow Karen Ristuccia heard about it and volunteered to write articles, explaining various distinctive elements of our mission and approach to education. Of course, since Karen was writing them, the articles were great, and they helped our parents and prospective parents understand what this new school was doing and why. Karen articulated how a school could combine the joy of a Charlotte Mason approach with the rigor of classical learning.

Those *Wilberforce Weekly* articles are what later became the chapters of this book, *Joyful Rigor*. These pages have helped countless parents and educators understand this unique and beautiful education. In those early days, we did not have a high school, yet. This new edition includes chapters explaining how joyful rigor has extended into our Upper School.

Sixteen years after the first articles were published, this new edition is printed in honor of Dr. Ristuccia's retirement from full-time service at Wilberforce. During her years at Wilberforce, Dr. Ristuccia has trained and mentored teachers, taught and inspired students, and encouraged and guided parents. We will miss her daily presence at Wilberforce greatly. This book, however, will be a tangible reminder of her enduring legacy in the lives of so many.

Howe Whitman Jr.
Head of School
The Wilberforce School

March 2021

Prologue

I suppose that *Joyful Rigor* seems like an odd title for a book (or for an educational philosophy, for that matter). Isn't "joyful rigor" an oxymoron? How can learning that is strict/ meticulous/accurate/precise (or any other synonym for "rigor") mesh with education that is delightful/thrilling/ pleasurable/ satisfying? Still, strange as it may seem, joyful rigor—a blend of academic challenges to mind and heart— is one of the chief goals for which The Wilberforce School strives and, by the grace of God, very often achieves. A young school in Princeton, New Jersey, The Wilberforce School (hereafter TWS) seeks to provide "a distinctively Christian education" in tandem with a methodology of joyful discovery. To achieve this hybrid, the founders of TWS looked to the writings of Charlotte Mason, a British educator of the late nineteenth and early twentieth centuries. Miss Mason believed that all children learned best when they were surrounded by rich ideas as revealed primarily in texts, artwork, nature, and music. Her writings gave form to the ideals expressed in the mission of TWS.

The founders of TWS not only carefully crafted its mission but also thoughtfully chose its school verse: "Finally, brothers, whatever is true, whatever is honorable, whatever is just, whatever is pure, whatever is lovely, whatever is commendable, if there is any excellence, if there is anything worthy of praise, think about these things" (Philippians 4:8). Since Paul wrote the letter to the Philippians while he was imprisoned in Rome, it is hard, at first, to understand the drumbeat of joy pounding throughout his epistle. Paul is not defeated by circumstances. Because he observes in the sacrificial giving and unstinting service of this Macedonian church the signs of God's handprint, Paul exalts: "Rejoice in the Lord always, and again I say rejoice!" (1:4). This command does not contradict the exhortation in 4:8 but instead demonstrates the fact that Paul sees no contradiction between a life of integrity, excellence, thoroughness, and dependability and a life of joy.

When the conditions are right, joy naturally accompanies academic rigor. On the other hand, minds focused on knowledge acquisition (when attempted for the goals of selfish gain and gratuitous entertainment) tend to stagnate, opting for the trivial, the banal, and the trite. Such an education may skirt happiness, but it completely misses joy. At TWS, joy is closely associated with the vital books, music, artwork, and outdoor experiences that occupy our interest. We reject those fluffy texts that patronize students, offering to them predigested ideas and mental junk food. Our students consume living books, listen to living music, and imitate living art. It is the reason that our students memorize and meditate on well-chosen poems and scripture passages that encase beautiful thoughts in beautiful words. It is why we recommit ourselves daily to habits of courtesy and kindness, modesty and integrity. It is the motivation behind our students' efforts to write, draw, and sing.

The chapters that follow illustrate how serious (should I say rigorous?) and yet how much fun (joy?) are our days at TWS. I begin my discussions with a definition of Christian education and then of classical Christian education. I then move on to consider how TWS experiences classical Christian education in the context of the Charlotte Mason methodology. Every teacher at TWS can tell you that Charlotte Mason pioneered teaching methods that took advantage of a child's natural curiosity and delight in discovery. At TWS, we believe that children learn best with a balanced approach that is both experiential and disciplined, that engages both the mind and the heart, that develops cognitive ability by igniting curiosity and passion. This book concludes with some thoughts about purposeful education, one that unites prayerful inquiry with an understanding of a biblical worldview and its implications on both scholarship and life.

We at TWS are educators of purpose. That purpose includes delighting in the struggle. It also includes sharing our vision and our story with those who also would choose to learn and teach in an atmosphere of "joyful rigor." It is a tremendous privilege to join with children as they discover ideas, grapple with realities, and conquer perplexities. Mental muscles are built by work, arduous but rewarding work. Joy comes through real successes and has much more value than would any mere "participation trophy." The Wilberforce School I write about is not perfect, either in the sense of flawless or in that of complete. It is a work in progress. It is work that we hope others will experience as well. TWS is a place where people (student scholars and teachers) excel in the delightful task of learning about God's world and their place within it. Come join us in this great adventure.

Our Philosophical Underpinnings

A Christian School?
Part One

A t the beginning of each school year, when the class three students look at their first Latin lesson, they will read and recite the following sentence: *"In principio erat verbum."* This quotation of John 1:1 comes from Jerome's Latin Vulgate and translates: "In the beginning was the Word." The Latin noun *"principium"* most often means "beginning." In the Middle Ages, the noun *"principium"* also came to take on a corollary meaning "foundation" or "principle." It seems only natural that a principal (that is I) would be interested in principles (that is, in the foundations on which we began The Wilberforce School). These facts, then—the meaning of *"principium,"* the homophone of "principal/principle," and the beginning of a new year—combine to elicit this first essay, as well as the ones that follow.

While each of us at The Wilberforce School (TWS) would affirm that our school rests on clear spiritual and pedagogical principles, many of us also would confess that sometimes we struggle to articulate these very principles. It is my hope and prayer that these essays will help each member of the TWS community to understand more deeply and embrace more fully the concepts that first excited us about the school. As a corollary, I hope that these explanations will inspire those outside the TWS circle to emulate and improve on our fusion of Charlotte Mason and classical Christian pedagogy.

Since we are discussing *"principia,"* it seems only natural to begin at the beginning. Emblazoned on the website of TWS, printed on our literature, and informing all that we do, our school proclaims itself a Christian institution. What does it mean that we are "Christian"? The book of Acts (11:26) relates that the disciples were first called Christians as an act of derision; it was as if someone were asking, "Who do these upstarts think they were anyway? Do they profess themselves to be 'little Christs'?" The moniker stuck and with it the inherent call—Christians are to imitate Christ.

First of all, then, TWS is founded on a belief in the gospel of Christ—a message of human frailty and divine triumph, of a world askew and a justifying God, of a redemptive community and a kingdom purpose. TWS is not "Christian" merely because of statements our parents and teachers sign or because of the books we read. We are "Christian" because we seek to live out daily and practically this stated faith, recognizing our students as bearers of God's image and accepting each believer's calling to study, develop, and serve our world so that God's glory will be seen and his kingdom promoted. It is no mean task that lies before us.

As a "Christian" school, TWS is defined not only by what it is—Christ affirming and Christ imitating—but also by what it is not—dualistic. Certain types of dualism are in vogue today. When I walked into the local Barnes & Noble last month, an entire table was devoted to Gnosticism, a dualistic faith that harkens back to the first century AD. What is dualism? It is a belief that a radical split exists between body and spirit, between flesh and mind, between human and divine. For the Gnostics, the earthly was too polluted to ever contact the heavenly. Gnosticism and Christianity are opposites. Christianity is steeped in incarnation, the "in-fleshing" of the holy Son, his union of human and divine realms. What is true about the Creator directs his creation. There are not two distinct truths—the one Lord reigns over all. As Dutch statesman Abraham Kuyper used to reiterate: "It is as if Christ said to us, 'This is my world, every inch of it.'" A contemporary restatement of this united reality is as follows: "There is not one molecule that is not God's."

It wasn't until I entered graduate school (for the first time, you who are laughing) that I realized with horror my predicament: I was at once a committed Christian and a practical dualist. On the one hand, I had my academic life, where I tried to "act Christianly" without "thinking Christianly." On the other hand, I had my spiritual life, where I worshipped my Lord and Savior. Jesus taught that no one can serve two masters. The Old Testament teaches that we are to love God with our whole soul, heart, mind, and strength. My approach to learning was fatally flawed; its dualism was foreign, false, and futile.

I am so glad that God delivered me from dualistic confusion. What an advantage that, from the outset, our students receive that which Francis Schaeffer termed "true Truth." TWS students acknowledge God's truth, in nature studies and mathematics, in history and art imitation, in copy work and recitation. Christian education is about authenticity and wholeness. What a privilege and what a humbling responsibility it is to partner with God and with our students' parents in this task!

A Christian School? Part Two

With my introductory Principium, we embarked on a study of *"principia,"* those underlying principles that characterize The Wilberforce School (TWS). Commencing with our "fundamental" foundation, I began to answer a question that is at once incredibly simple and vastly profound: What does it mean for TWS to be a "Christian" school? In effect, I responded that "since Christians are people who imitate Christ, a Christian school is an educational institution made up of teachers and students who seek to imitate Christ while pursuing a holistic curriculum in which all truth is God's." Of course, to define a Christian school fully, much more could be said. Here, I will discuss two additional components of a genuinely Christian school: God-ward accountability and God-directed mission.

Anyone who has been reading business materials from the last fifteen years knows that neither accountability nor mission is a concept unique to Christian schools. The concept of "no child left behind" is so well known that in a 2006 *New York Times* article a scientist lamented Pluto's demotion from planetary status, saying that the new standard was "no ice ball left behind." In many states, both funding and teacher salary levels are tied to performance on standardized tests. States such as California and Texas issue lists of approved textbooks for all their localities. Real estate decisions are often based on the average SAT scores of students in the local public schools. Clearly, accountability is in. The issue is not whether there is any accountability but rather to what or to whom is the school accountable? In the Christian school, the answer to this accountability question is neither the federal government, nor the state department of education, nor the housing market. As the apostle Paul explains in Ephesians, Christians are part of a living, growing body, one that Jesus Christ himself heads. He is the authority for all we do (4:15–16).

A truly Christian school community unites parents, teachers, staff, and students, who all regularly reaffirm their submission to Christ's leadership, purposes, and example. In Matthew 28:18–20, Christ proclaims that his absolute authority authenticates and empowers his great commission. We who are in the disciple-making business (which is, of course, the essence of Christian education) do well to remember that God's purposes must occur both by his power and according to his prescription. For this reason, Christian school teachers recognize and promote parents as the primary educators and disciple-makers of children (cf. Deut. 6:5–9). Unlike the New Jersey public school principal I know who routinely includes in his "back-to-school night" speech the assertion that he knows more about, and can better counsel, any given junior higher than could that child's parents, truly Christian teachers and administrators refuse to demean, underrate, or dismiss parental accountability. God's appointments are never trivial.

Now let's talk about mission: For what exactly are Christian schools accountable? What constitutes a divinely directed Christian education? In his gospel, Luke describes Christ's educational experience from the ages of two to twelve thus: "And the child [Jesus] grew and became strong, filled with wisdom. And the favor of God was upon him" (2:40). It was this type of education that prompted the Father to announce his pleasure in his Son at the baptism (Luke 3:22). Our mission as Christian school educators is to partner with parents and church in equipping our students to be willing servants of God, set apart for his kingdom. Our students need to develop physically, mentally, and spiritually. This is why the *Parent-Student Handbook* of TWS discusses matters as disparate as healthy snacks and reconciliation, proper dress, and moral habits. We are concerned with the total child, knowing that we are preparing students not merely for adulthood but also for eternity.

Our school is Christian to the extent that its members prove Christian—in creed and in practice, in hope and in prayer. Now, this exacting standard brings up what our

Victorian friends called a "sticky wicket." Christians often fail to act like Christians. Too often, in fact, we act just like those around us. Calling a school "Christian" offers no guarantee against rudeness, gossip, injustice, or misunderstanding. Nor does it promise that school personnel do not, at times, act either autonomously or randomly. All these offenses can and do occur.

In light of this "sticky wicket," Christians must exhibit humility. Christian schools must promote humility. Christian school community will soon decay unless the community members follow God's pattern for repentance, reconciliation, and restoration. It is a sad—but true—fact that all human beings are finite, frail, and flawed. This observation lies behind the motto of TWS, which is *"Gratia et Veritas."* A Christian school needs the truth (*"veritas"*), but it also desperately needs grace (*"gratia"*). The truth about the Christian school's participation in, and accountability for, its discipleship mission will only motivate and not paralyze to the degree we permit God's forgiving grace to enable, encourage, and empower our service.

A Classical Christian School? (The What)

Now that I have devoted two Principia to talking about what it means for a school to be a "Christian school," I want to move on to discuss another adjective that describes The Wilberforce School (TWS): the word "classical." If you read at all about classical schools, you will have discovered that the word "classical" has many connotations, not all of which describe TWS. Alternately, classical education can describe learning focused on Greek and Roman culture, learning that meets certain established and traditionally authoritative standards (such as teaching the Great Books), and learning that is formal, objective, balanced, and timeless. When we call the education at TWS "classical," we particularly allude to its content, its methodology, and its design.

TWS education is classical in its content, both in the materials studied and in the arrangement of those materials. With regard to the materials studied, TWS concentrates on Western history, literature, art, and music, using the West as a lens through which to understand the non-Western world. We also study Latin, a classical language from which derives approximately half the words in contemporary English. We study this carefully chosen content in an orderly fashion, moving systematically, although the systems vary with the discipline. In history, for example, we may move chronologically, studying a culture through time, or geographically, moving from city to state to country to continent and beyond. This emphasis on a logical presentation of material is another classical trademark.

TWS education is also classical in its methodology, in that we use traditional, proven teaching methods such as recitation, dictation, narration, and art and composition imitation. While I will not here review the philosophical and historical context that accompanied the abandonment of classical education's proven educational methodology, I acknowledge that just such abandonment did occur in twentieth-century America. In is ironic that it has taken the success of Suzuki music instruction for American educators to acknowledge the wisdom of memorization, recitation, and imitation. The rigors and joys of classical education never became obsolete, whereas many of the promises of progressive education have proven empty.

Finally, TWS education is classical in its design, in that it uses the Trivium both as a developmental model for approaching a subject and as a system for teaching any given "chunk" of classical content. Many of you recall encountering the Trivium before—it is a common theme of classical Christian educators, who often point to Dorothy Sayers' essay, "The Lost Tools of Learning," as their inspiration. As a review of some basic understandings, recall that *"trivium"* is Latin for "three roads" or "ways" and that this educational triumvirate has served as a pedagogical model throughout most of Western history. According to the Trivium, students fall into distinct developmental stages that dictate three different teaching roads: the grammar stage, the logic stage, and the rhetoric stage. Students in the grammar stage particularly enjoy acquiring facts (the "grammars" of particular disciplines); those in the logic stage enjoy debating and evaluating acquired facts; and those in the rhetoric stage enjoy appropriating and applying what they have learned and debated. TWS students are divided between the grammar and logic stages. While it would be incorrect to say that these students do not appropriate and apply their lessons, current TWS students spend the greatest proportion of their day learning the facts, rules, and relationships concerned with their various academic disciplines.

The Trivium not only provides a model for teaching students of diverse ages, but this "three roads" approach also provides a paradigm for teaching any particular subject. This is why classical schools teach their students not only about the grammars of their academic disciplines but also about their controversies and implications. When a student begins a study of Civil War history, he or she starts by learning some facts (a "grammar"). These facts include the meaning of states' rights, secession, and abolition. Beyond a list of facts, though, the student must move on if he or she is to understand the forces leading to the Civil War (logic material), the strategies that governed this war (logic material), and the long-lasting implications of this war (rhetoric material). While individual students are developmentally best suited to one level of the Trivium, all students must make forays out of their developmental "comfort zone" in order to gain not only knowledge but also wisdom and understanding.

I have spent a lot of time answering the "What?" question, but so far I have ignored the "Why?" question. Why classically educate? Why pair classical education with Christian education? But I have written enough for one sitting. For the rationale behind classical and Christian education, we will have to wait for Principium 4.

A Classical Christian School? (The Why)

With the increasing popularity of classical Christian education, you may be surprised to learn that over the years, many people have questioned whether or not an educational system could be at once "classical" and "Christian." Back in the late second and early third centuries, Church Father Tertullian (AD 160–225) considered the classical-Christian interrelationship and concluded: "What indeed has Athens to do with Jerusalem?" For Tertullian, then, a Christian education that focuses on seeking "simplicity of heart" is diametrically opposed to a classical education that concentrates instead on amassing philosophical argumentation. The Bible demonstrates a similar uneasiness with classical education when it emphasizes primarily knowledge acquisition. Thus Paul speaks of unbelievers who while "claiming to be wise" become "fools" (Romans 1:22), of natural persons who find the "things of the Spirit of God" to be incomprehensible (1 Cor. 2:14), and of the wisdom of this world that is "folly with God" (1 Cor. 3:19).

A narrow understanding of "classical education"—one focusing only on the pedagogical practices of Ancient Greece and Rome—is no fitting partner for Christian education. But there are different understandings of "classical education," ones that focus on gaining wisdom in the context of truth, goodness, and beauty. Such classical education accords well with the Christian worldview. In fact, this type of classical education sounds so right because its origin is not the philosophers of Ancient Greece, Ancient Rome, and the Middle Ages but instead the mind of this world's Designer. Jesus spoke of himself as "the Way, the Truth, and the Life" (John 14:6). In other words, Jesus embodied the Trivium. As the Way, he offered the "grammar" for living. As the Truth, he exhibited the standard for experience, the "logic" against which to measure all other truths, rules, and forms. As the Life, he demonstrated the wholeness and unity of wise thinking, speaking, doing, and worshipping.

The pattern of knowledge (the acquisition of both particular facts and basic principles), understanding (the ability to discern, interpret, and evaluate knowledge), wisdom (the capacity to synthesize, apply, extend, and incorporate understanding) has come down to us as the educational mode called the "Trivium." Make no mistake, though, the Bible linked these ideas together long before the Greeks, the medieval

Scholastics, or contemporary classical educators did. Recall, for example, these three verses from Proverbs:

- "Buy truth, and do not sell it; buy wisdom, and instruction, and understanding" (23:23).
- "By wisdom a house is built, and by understanding it is established. By knowledge the rooms are filled with all precious and pleasant riches" (24:3, 4)
- "For the Lord gives wisdom; from his mouth come knowledge and understanding" (2:6).

We have arrived at the answer to our question: Why adopt the classical education paradigm? The reason we at TWS choose to classically educate is because this paradigm reflects the nature of both human beings and the created world. We desire an education for time and eternity, not merely to further the economic machine. True education is not only about skills training, nor simply about utilitarian equipping for career advancement. Such a truncated view of education produces a desire for facts and power rather than for goodness and wisdom. History (and contemporary life) afford us many examples of people who were informed but not wise (and so manipulated information for their purposes) or who were powerful but not good (and so led nations to horrible ends). Facts without discretion, power without holiness—that is the legacy of a soulless education torn apart from its roots. The type of classical education TWS espouses is one that reflects and honors the Source of all knowledge, understanding, and wisdom: "O the depths of the riches and wisdom and knowledge of God. How unsearchable are his judgments and how inscrutable his ways! For who has known the mind of the Lord, and who has been his counselor? For from him and through him and to him are all things. To him be glory forever!" (Romans 11:33–36).

A Charlotte Mason Flavor

After writing four Principia devoted to defining how a school could be both a "Christian" and a "classical" school, I now move to a third modifier (a phrase, in fact) that describes The Wilberforce School (TWS). According to all our literature, TWS culture displays "a Charlotte Mason influence." These words call to mind the instruction and example of Charlotte Mason, a British educator who lived from 1842 to 1923.

Charlotte Mason spoke and wrote about both educational practice and the philosophy behind that practice. From the age of sixteen onward, Charlotte (this first name familiarity might be a horror in Victorian England but seems the norm for twenty-first-century people speaking about Miss Mason and her work) was involved in education first as a student working toward her First Class Teaching Certificate and then as a classroom teacher, a curriculum writer, a home education supervisor, and a teacher trainer. In addition, Charlotte's lectures on home education led to the formation of the Parents National Education Union (PNEU), a group that forwarded Charlotte's thought and published a periodical entitled, *The Parents Review*. In 1891, Charlotte moved to Ambleside, England (in the Lake District), and founded an educational training school that she named "The House of Education" (today, Charlotte Mason College). She also began a small elementary school, where her teachers could see the Mason methodology used with real children in real classrooms. Today, Charlotte Mason's six-volume study on education has been reprinted (Amazon or its competitors would be glad to sell you a copy), and her legacy of education "for the children's sake" continues in many places, including our own.

When we speak of a "Charlotte Mason influence," do not suppose that Charlotte's touch at TWS is either faint or occasional. Rather, Charlotte's influence pervades every discipline, assignment, and conversation. This is so first of all because Charlotte Mason was a committed Christian whose allegiance to her Maker guided all she did. Along this line, Charlotte repeatedly reminded her followers that all children are made in God's image ("persons" is Charlotte's term) and that, as such, children must not be sentimentalized, manipulated, abused, dismissed, or discounted. Remember that Charlotte was writing in a day when children were relegated to governesses, told to be seen and not heard, enslaved in factories, and beaten at school. Charlotte's words were both radical and life-giving.

Charlotte Mason argued that just as children must not be trivialized or brutalized, so also they must not be romanticized, sentimentalized, pampered, or worshipped. Children were sinners, often giving in to their weaknesses or choosing incorrectly owing to their ignorance. Teachers then serve as mentors, especially by transmitting habits that would fortify these scholars so that they could make correct choices and act wisely.

At TWS, the Charlotte Mason influence is broad. It appears in poetry memorization, in art imitation, and in composer and picture study. It motivates nature walks, nature drawing, and nature study. It reminds us to read only "living books" (robust, uplifting, time-tested works) and avoid "twaddle" (Charlotte's word for "dumbed-down" literature). Daily we at TWS demonstrate that classical education is enriched and enlarged when flavored with a Charlotte Mason influence.

There is much to say about Charlotte's teaching, but I will make only a few comments at this juncture. In each case we can see how a Charlotte Mason "influence" improved on the classical framework that characterized the education of her day:

- Traditionally, classical education emphasizes written narration from the earliest grades; a Charlotte Mason influence underscores the importance of literature while focusing on perfecting oral narration in the earliest years and progressing naturally to written narrations (i.e., compositions).

- Traditionally, classical education emphasizes academic rigor; a Charlotte Mason influence adds to this rigor (what Charlotte terms a student's "life's work") an atmosphere of joyful discovery.

- Traditionally, classical education emphasizes training in virtue; Charlotte Mason stresses the development of Christian character through (among other means) habituation and study of historical examples.

- Traditionally, classical education emphasizes rote memory; Charlotte Mason focuses on memory of poetry, speeches, and also the narration (after only one reading) of sections from great literature.

Charlotte Mason was a committed Christian who herself was educated along classical lines. She wanted children from all social and economic strata to experience a rich, idea-filled education. A Charlotte Mason influence produces an education that is both practical and powerful. If a visitor were to join TWS's morning assembly he or she would hear the students echo the PNEU motto ("I am, I can, I ought, I will"), This motto accurately and succinctly captures the transformation possible when children experience in all their academic endeavors the flavor of Charlotte Mason pedagogy.

Education as Discipline

As the years passed and her fame spread, Charlotte Mason was asked repeatedly to summarize her philosophy. Her answer was fourfold: "Education is an atmosphere, a discipline, a life, and a science of relations." Here, we will look at the second of those descriptions: "Education is a discipline." Early in her teaching career, Charlotte Mason discovered that while her young charges were whole persons who loved to learn, explore, and discover, their knowledge acquisition could not ensure success either in school or in life. Being weak and uninformed, young students often failed to grow wise even as they became more educated. Charlotte Mason longed to discover a tool to help students to overcome this seeming inertia.

Thus Charlotte continued to experiment and observe until she realized that the key to lifelong educational success was harnessing the power of habit. A "habit" is an activity that is performed so regularly that it becomes easy (or at least easier), customary, or even automatic. We are all glad that we now perform such routine tasks as brushing our teeth, tying our shoes, and buttoning our coats much more rapidly and effectively than we did when we first learned those skills. Habits come in many forms. Some of us have the habit of praying before meals; others of us do not. Some of us throw away junk mail immediately, whereas others of us wait for a significant pileup before we perform that task. Some of us react first to stress with panic and then prayer; others of us reverse that order.

Habits can be good or bad. Regular exercise is a good habit, whereas biting one's nails is less esteemed. Charlotte Mason understood that when a teacher or parent failed to instill good habits, often the result was that bad habits were reinforced. Charlotte found metaphor to epitomize the power and perversity of habit. Habit, she wrote, is "like fire" in that it is "a bad master but an indispensable servant." For this reason, she felt it a shame when "life was not duly eased for us by those [parents and teachers] whose business it was to lay down lines of habit upon which our behavior might run easily" (*Philosophy of Education,* p. 101). She again compared habits to railroad lines, saying that "lines of habit must be laid down. . . if we fail to lay down lines of right thinking and acting, the opposite lines will fix themselves of their own accord" (*Philosophy of Education,* pp. 99, 101).

Charlotte also understood that habit formation was far easier and less painful than habit reformation, so she enjoined parents and teachers, from a child's earliest days, to devote themselves to effective training in habits. This meant, in turn, that parents and teachers be watchful (ensuring that the habits be practiced regularly), considerate (endeavoring to explain each habit's importance), and consistent (unwavering both in example and in encouragement). Habituation was crucial. Charlotte correctly observed: "Whether or not you choose to take any trouble about the formation of habits, it is habit, all the same, that governs 99 percent of a child's actions" (*Home Education*, p. 110).

At The Wilberforce School (TWS), we have heeded Charlotte's strong words about habit. Beginning in the first days of school, we help our students to appreciate and develop habits of study (such as attentiveness, thoroughness, and diligence), of person (such as neatness, organization, and modesty), and of character (such as respect, kindness, and integrity). While we recognize that the Christian life is one of grace and not works, we also affirm that the longer a believer follows Christ, the more that believer's life should resemble Christ's. We are seeking, in other words, to develop habits of godliness even more than habits of study. When the apostle Paul wrote to Timothy, Paul said: "Train yourself for godliness; for while bodily training is of some value, godliness is of value in every way, as it holds promise for the present life and also for the life to come" (1 Timothy 4:8).

Training in habit is important, but it must never degenerate to mere external performance. As Charlotte Mason reiterated, effective training in habit focuses on building up persons. It involves relationship and responsibility and not achievement and control. It produces peace and confidence and not comparison and conformity. It is the work of disciples and mentors, not of flatterers and show-offs.

Good habits are wonderful once a person acquires them, but the process of acquisition often proves slow, awkward, and uncomfortable. People who make a study of such processes conclude that it takes a minimum of six weeks of daily practice to acquire even the simplest new habit. No wonder the "New Year's resolution" has become a joke. So often we lack endurance and perspective, perseverance and hope. Education is indeed a "discipline." As such, in time and by God's grace, it yields not only knowledge but also wisdom and righteousness and joy.

Education as Atmosphere

I n the last Principium, I began to analyze the second of the characteristics enumerated in Charlotte Mason's fourfold definition of education: "Education is an atmosphere, a discipline, a life, and a science of relations." Here, I will continue the analysis by focusing on her first statement: "Education is an atmosphere."

After Charlotte had spent several years studying education, she concluded that a teacher's most critical responsibility is to create an atmosphere (what she termed a "thought-environment") in which students' minds will be exercised and their hearts nurtured. Crafting such an environment is a two-pronged proposition: Teachers must both reject certain practices and adopt other ones. Charlotte spoke negatively of those educational atmospheres that sought to control student behavior and performance through didactics and guilt manipulation, through intense competition and comparison, through overtesting and relentless grading, through rigidity and unremitting drill, or alternately, through coddling and overprotection.

If we are honest with ourselves, we adults (parents and teachers) sometimes have been guilty of these very "toxic atmosphere" practices. At times, when talking to (or about) our students/children, we have caught ourselves uttering such unhealthy statements as these:

- "After all I do for you in making dinner, you should at least set the table without grumbling."
- "Good students do not throw food."
- "Why can't you be more like your sister?"
- "Don't mind John's crankiness; he's too tired to be polite."

Whether it occurs in the home or in the classroom, a healthy, heart-nurturing atmosphere is no accident. In fact, if the teachers do not consciously create the right kind of atmosphere, wrong kinds of atmospheres descend on classrooms as weeds do in a garden. We who lead must guard our attitudes and words. We must model and mentor mature choices, careful speech, and personal responsibility. Thankfully, Charlotte Mason provided us with specific help as to how to create a positive atmosphere, one in which all children are challenged to grow in their knowledge of God, of their classmates, and of the world that God has entrusted to them.

The Wilberforce School (TWS) takes seriously Charlotte's suggestions for creating a positive classroom atmosphere. For example, following her advice, we devote the morning hours to some of the day's hardest work. This leaves the afternoons for such activities as nature study, reading aloud, and composer and picture study. In addition, we take seriously Charlotte's life rule: "Never be within doors when you can rightly be without" (*Home Education*, p. 42). Whether the venue is recess, snack time, physical education class, or nature study, we take advantage of the beauty, diversity, and interest of God's world—his expansive and ever-changing classroom.

TWS also incorporates other ideas from Charlotte Mason about creating a positive classroom atmosphere. We seek to provide students with academic challenges without over-pressuring them and to allow students freedom of choice within the routines of their well-ordered classroom. When you visit TWS, you will see students quietly leaving their desks to sharpen a pencil, pick out a book to read, visit the nature table, or hand in a paper. You also will see students stretched as they seek to meet personal goals, both academic and personal.

Charlotte Mason understood the connotation of "home" even more than do the modern marketers of "estate homes." She believed that the best classrooms were "homelike" in the highest sense of that word. Homelike classrooms are ones that are inviting and restful. When you visit TWS, you discover this type of classroom. In one room, you will hear beautiful music playing; in another, you will see students sitting on the rug listening to and narrating back a story. Classroom pets—from fish to gerbils to geckos—attract your eye, as do healthy plants, classic art prints, living books, tasteful time-lines, careful artwork, and inspiring quotations. And if our students saw you, they would greet you warmly and even ask a sincere, "How are you?"

Homes are not static. They are places of growth and strug-gle, comfort and reconciliation. As beautiful as any art print is the sight of a line-leader holding the door, of two students apologizing and shaking hands, of a class sharing a joke or clapping for someone's hard-won accomplishment. TWS is not a perfect place, but it is the perfect place for persons to learn and laugh, to invent and imagine, to sing and sketch, to run and rest. Pervading it all is our profound gratitude to God. He nurtures us so that we can nurture others. He welcomes us so that we welcome others. He makes his home in our hearts so that we can from our hearts offer refuge to others.

Education as Both Life and a Science of Relations

Again, I continue my consideration of Charlotte Mason's fourfold definition of education: "Education is an atmosphere, a discipline, a life, and a science of relations." Here, I will conclude the analysis by discussing education as both "a life" and "a science of relations."

While the statement "Education is life" sounds pithy, what does this truism actually mean? When Charlotte Mason made this statement, she was not primarily describing physical life but instead the life of the inner person—the life of the mind and soul. In defining physical life, scientists often list a variety of characteristics; a representative sampling would include metabolism, reproduction, growth, and movement. The life of the mind consists of a parallel list of characteristics. As with the physical person, the inner person needs "food." Charlotte explains, therefore: "The mind feeds on ideas" (*Home Education*, Preface). Just as physical bodies grow and develop, so critically thinking minds continue both to generate new ideas and to expose new facets of existing ideas. An active mind is one that welcomes diverse perspectives, that seeks broad-ranging applications, and that generates new concepts that can, in turn, grow and develop. This type of mind assesses, evaluates, harnesses, amends, and expands. Powerful ideas resist the status quo.

Charlotte Mason was a philosopher, to be sure, but she was always a practical one. For this reason, she outlined both those educational choices which promote mental life and those which lead to mental decay. Just as physical bodies grow best with healthy, enriching food, so the inner person develops best in the presence of invigorating, uplifting ideas. For this reason, Charlotte insisted that students be nurtured on the best in art, music, and literature. Charlotte even coined the term "living books" to describe those life-giving works, either fiction or nonfiction, that are well written, interesting, informative, imaginative, challenging, and enjoyable.

If we want students to be mentally and spiritually robust, we can no more think for them than we could eat for them if we wanted them to be physically nourished. Too often teachers fail to trust their students to attend to, evaluate, and then respond to ideas. (You should be hearing echoes of the Trivium at this moment.) Students do not crave pre-digested material; they want to sink their mental teeth into nourishing, rich, and appetizing mind food. This is why the classrooms at The Wilberforce School (TWS) are replete with dictionaries, charts, manuals, art prints, music CDs, math manipulatives, and full-length books. We expect our students to dig and discover, to weigh and wonder, to search and select, and to appraise and apply.

If the mind can be enlivened, it also can be deadened. Junk mind food—what Charlotte calls "twaddle"—can dull a student's appetite for the good, the pure, and the beautiful; so too can insipid activities, needless repetition, illogical unit studies (such as counting mangers in math because it is Christmas time), and overuse of drill and lecture. Even room design can deaden attention and promote mental hunger. When classroom walls are swollen with frill and fluff, students view their room as a place for entertainment and amusement rather than for exploration and reflection. Teachers must give students tools, space, and time so that students experience genuine "Eureka!" moments. True education forwards an abundant inner life.

The ideas that make up educational life are more than ephemera and dreams; they are stances for relating to God and his world. This is why Charlotte Mason added a fourth description—"science of relations"—to what she designed originally as a three-point definition of education. Today, when we hear the word "science," we think of natural science, of the compilation and interpretation of data to explain how the world works. When Charlotte Mason spoke of science, she was speaking of "systemized knowledge." Charlotte believed that learning unites a web of facts and ideas, understandings, and responses. In speaking about history, for example, Charlotte stated: "Every child is an heir to an enormous patrimony, heir to all ages, inheritor of all the present" (1902 PNEU Conference paper, p. 485). Education, then, encompasses all the relationships a student has, whether with God, with family and friends, with historical figures and fictional characters, with authors and builders, with math tables and marching bands, with gerbils and pine trees, with soccer balls and knitting needles, or with teachers and coaches.

Charlotte Mason understood that education could only be life-giving and relationship-building if it had the correct center. She explained: "This idea of all education springing from and resting on our relation to Almighty God is one which we have ever labored to enforce. . . . the culmination of all education is that personal knowledge of and intimacy with God" (*School Education*, p. 95). We who are made in the image of God were made for life and relationship. We are made to thrive in an atmosphere of authority and accountability, of discipline and devotion, of information and ideas, and of connections and caring. Atmosphere, discipline, life, relationship—education means drawing students out and leading them toward the fullness God intended them to achieve. By his grace, we at TWS will strive to prove educators according to Charlotte's full definition of that word.

FUNDAMENTALLY CHARLOTTE MASON

Narration

Whenever anyone writes or speaks about a "Charlotte Mason education," two words appear repeatedly: one is "habit," and the other is "narration." Since I already discussed habituation as part of my consideration of education as discipline, I am naturally led to consider what Miss Mason meant when she spoke of narration as her preferred method of instruction.

"Narration"—a word that means retelling the particulars of a story, event, or concept—is as old as speech itself. Obviously, then, Charlotte Mason did not invent narration, nor was she the first to bring this technique into the classroom. But Miss Mason gave such a primary place to narration and she so developed and applied it that she ended up with a newer, richer, more powerful understanding of the word. In the Charlotte Mason classroom, narration most often means telling back the words and concepts that have first been read to the student from a "living book" of either fiction or nonfiction. After the teacher reads the passage once (and he or she never rereads), the narration begins. In successive turns, students strive to tell back everything they have heard, even to the point of using some of the rich vocabulary that the passage includes. They seek to employ the author's own language, cadences, sequencing, and details. The goal of narration is accurate and complete retelling; students are neither to summarize nor embellish. Through narration, students both accurately recall content and begin to understand and apply that content.

Becoming expert in narration is a process. Novice Explorers (Junior Kindergarten students) tell back two or three sentences at a time; by the time they are in class four, students can narrate multiple pages proficiently. Charlotte Mason describes a narration lesson involving eight-year-olds as follows:

> The reading should be consecutive from a well-chosen book. Before the reading for the day begins, the teacher should talk a little (and get the children to talk) about the last lessons with a few words about what is to be read in order that the children may be animated by expectation, but she should beware of explanation and especially of forestalling the narrative. Then she may read two or three pages, enough to include the episode; after that let her call up the children to narrate, in turns, if there be several of them. They not only narrate with spirit and accuracy, but succeed in conveying the style of their author [*Home Education*, pp. 232–233].

Earliest narrations are oral; later ones are often written in the form of a composition. Sometimes students narrate by acting out a scene or by illustrating in pictures what they have heard. Once students learn to narrate verbal material, they begin narrating other material—paintings and sculpture, science diagrams from manuals, interesting life experiences, mathematical story problems, and even musical compositions. In most cases, The Wilberforce School (TWS) students have so quickly become accomplished at narration that their teachers (and parents) stand both astonished and humbled.

Why did Miss Mason so often propose the narration method? First of all, because listening to (and then narrating back) either great literature or informative nonfiction proves an enjoyable and effective way to develop attention. Developing attention, in turn, is a key to being a good student, a good scientist, and a good friend. Narration also helps students to make material their own. As content is narrated, students discover a second opportunity to think about that content, to file it into their long-term memory, and to compare old and new ideas. Students also have a chance to dwell on beautiful language, wrestle with complex ideas, and trace out narrative connections. Teachers who use narration extensively have discovered that their students can remember narrated material months after it was first encountered.

When students develop their narration ability, they are, in turn, strengthening their mental powers. The ability to focus, to understand and connect details, and to put concepts into words increases a student's comprehension abilities.

These important skills are useful in every academic endeavor. Moreover, whether the discipline is botany, art history, or literary analysis, students cannot interpret what they have not first observed. Narration forces a student to slow down and attend, to notice big and little details, and to move beyond merely decoding words to genuine comprehension. Effective narration becomes the springboard for new questions and theories, leading then to more reading and more narration. As part of a cycle of joyful discovery, narration never need become dreary or routine.

For the classroom teacher, narration also serves as an excellent assessment tool. When a student tells back what he or she has heard, the teacher can assess the extent of his or her understanding of the material covered. Narration is also a key step in the student's development of higher-order thinking skills. Knowing and comprehending what one hears is prerequisite to correctly applying, analyzing, synthesizing, and evaluating that material.

If you were to visit TWS at any hour of the day, you probably would find some group of students in the process of narrating. During the day, students narrate Bible passages and historical novels, poems and pictures, hymns and timelines. Everyone loves a good story, and our students are no exception. They would be glad to share a few of those stories with you as well.

Nature Study

Another of the key features of a Charlotte Mason educa-tion is its emphasis on in-depth, firsthand nature study. Charlotte Mason felt that students should daily experience the natural world and weekly participate in a longer nature walk. Why this emphasis on natural observation and enjoy-ment? The preeminent answer to this question is found in the Bible. Nature has a message to proclaim. Psalm 19:1–2 tells us: "The heavens declare the glory of God, and the sky above proclaims his handiwork. Day to day pours out speech, and night to night reveals knowledge." If we want our children to glorify God, we must allow them to linger long in nature's school.

Nature study was a popular pastime in Charlotte Mason's day, but it has fallen on hard times. In his book, *Lost Child in the Woods: Saving Our Children from Nature-Deficit Disorder*, Richard Louw describes how forces such as overscheduling, threats of lawsuits (recently, several states have outlawed the playing of tag during school recess), criminalization of play in public parks, extreme environmental activism, tempting indoor activities (particularly television and computer games), and fear of strangers all have conspired to make outdoor play inadvisable, dangerous, or impossible. The bleakness of this situation multiplies, Louw continues, when one considers the growing body of scientific evidence indicating "that direct exposure to nature is essential for physical and emotional health" (pp. 13–14).

We at The Wilberforce School (TWS) are grateful that we have both a curricular incentive for and a perfect locale in which to experience nature study. Surrounded by trees, abutting a river, and just a crosswalk away from a canal pathway, we are blessed indeed. Over the years, we have spotted turtles and fish, birds and small mammals. We have sketched trees, leaves, fungi, and even the ubiquitous poison ivy (which sports some lovely shades in the fall). We have developed our abilities to use our eyes and our ears, our sense of smell, and—through drawing and painting in our nature journals—our sense of touch. We are learning to identify birds not only by color but also by habitat, flight, and call.

Our woods prove home to ibises and mallards, herons and eagles. One day a student spotted a hummingbird. At other times, students have collected leaves from the ground and returned to their field guides to identify oak and sassafras, maple and elm. A highlight was the day that after talking about the upcoming reading of *The Wind in the Willows*, Class One students saw a real mole!

Since science is the study of the natural world, not surprisingly, nature study provides a ready opportunity to introduce the various components of the scientific method, particularly researching, questioning, stating a hypothesis, experimenting, collecting and then interpreting data, and reaching a conclusion. Through their nature walks, their jotting of field notes, their sketches, and their pouring over of reference materials, TWS students research in the field of life science, collect data, and then interpret those data. Students soon learn that they cannot correctly interpret data unless they have first carefully observed their subjects and then thoroughly recorded their observations.

Inside the classroom, specimens from our nature tables help students to recognize patterns, generate hypotheses, and continually ask the all-important "why" questions. Some classes even spend time observing class pets. At different times, our classes have hosted many animal friends, including a rat, several fish, a gecko, a bird, and a hissing cockroach.

In *Home Education*, Charlotte Mason devotes an entire section (about one-sixth of her book) to the "Out-Door Life of Children." Her ideas run the gamut from having meals out of doors (a precedent for our snack times and noontime picnics) to painting pictures, from visiting various habitats to cultivating gardens, from hiking up mountains to identifying species, and from climbing rocks to relaxing in natural venues. All this time spent in the natural world introduces students to the value of conservation; to the order, intricacy, and design of God's creation; and to the power of natural beauty to motivate and inspire. No wonder Miss Mason associated many benefits with nature study; these include a greater reverence for life, a firsthand knowledge of animal and plant classification, an incentive for reading and using science books, and a blossoming of tranquility and joy.

Of course, a person need not restrict nature study only to school hours; one can enjoy the out-of-doors at any time of day. Together, families can celebrate the passing of seasons; the beauties of the night sky; the fun of feeding birds, pressing wildflowers, observing bees, or naming trees; and even the adventure of camping in the woods. Psalm 104 teaches that God designed this world as a showcase for his strength and wisdom and that our proper response to such knowledge is worship: "May the glory of the Lord endure forever! . . . I will sing to the Lord as long as I live; I will sing praise to my God while I have being" (Psalms 104:31–32). We at TWS desire that our nature study will continually generate similar God-directed praise wherever it occurs.

Using "Living Books"

At The Wilberforce School (TWS), Charlotte Mason's educational philosophy inspires us in many ways. For example, daily we heed her injunction to read and discuss "living books." According to Miss Mason, "living books" are whole books that exhibit imagination, emotion, and originality. These books are worthy because they unite careful expression with clear thinking. For Miss Mason, "living books" both exude life and expand life: "They [children] must grow up upon the best. . . . There is never a time when they are unequal to worthy thoughts, well put; inspiring tales, well told. Let Blake's 'Songs of Innocence' represent their standard in poetry, DeFoe and Stevenson, in prose; and we shall train a race of readers who will demand literature—that is, the fit and beautiful expression of inspiring ideas and pictures of life" (*Parents and Children*, p. 263).

On the subject of "living books," I think an expanded definition is in order. According to *Curriculum Guide* at

TWS: "Living books are characterized by powerful elevated language, vivid and engaging presentation of the human condition, artistic and captivating illustrations, clear message and purpose, expert knowledge of subject matter and themes, and ideas and incidents which spark argument, conversation, imagination, and/or curiosity." Karen Andreola, long-time student of the Charlotte Mason philosophy, offers these helps for recognizing such life-transforming, quality literature: "Living books. . . enliven the imagination of a child. . . . [These books] do not talk down to a child's level or omit odd and interesting vocabulary. . . . How can you recognize a living book. . . . see if it promotes noble thoughts rather than a jaded or misleading outlook on life. . . [give] the one-page test. Start reading. . . . You will know it's a living book when you hear them beg, 'Read me more!'" (*Practical Homeschooling*, p. 6, 1994).

Are you still a bit confused? Then here are some questions to ask when you evaluate a book's worthiness: Does it display both quality writing and well-developed ideas? Will it speak to a child's intellectual curiosity while also touching his or her heart? Does the book offer language and content that a child will enjoy narrating? Does the book discuss key cultural themes or images (such as the Trojan horse, Robin Hood, the struggle for freedom and justice, or Saul and David)? Remember as well, the standard of "living books" is not to strangle but to liberate. Why read Babysitters' Club books when one can read Lucy Maud Montgomery (*Anne of Green Gables*); why read *Goosebumps* or *Captain Underpants* when the riches of George MacDonald and Beatrix Potter await?

The world of living fiction is rich and varied. I'll just give a few examples here. Marguerite De Angeli provides excellent historical fiction (such as *Door in the Wall* and *Thee Hannah*) as she travels with her readers to locales as diverse as a farm in pre–Civil War Pennsylvania or a manor in Medieval England. Her stories depict real life, its ups and downs, triumphs and disappointments. Patricia St. John adventures (such as *The Runaway* and *Treasures in the Snow*) combine the various loves of this British nurse turned courageous North African missionary. St. John writes about the real trials children face in learning to love, forgive, trust, and sacrifice. Arthur Ransome's delightful stories (such as *Swallowdale*, and *Swallows and Amazons*) expose the author's love of sailing in the English Lake District, as well as his commitment to view children as full persons, with real trials and genuine successes. A master of word pictures, Ransome illustrates the joy of nature and of true community.

"Living books" need not be fictional. Consider, for instance, Jeanne Bendick's science biographies (such as *Archimedes and the Door of Science* and *Galen and the Gateway to Medicine*). In her books, Bendick weaves together mathematical and/or scientific principles into an enchanting story format. These books delight while leading naturally to further research and discovery. As for history, Genevieve Foster's narrative histories (such as *Augustus Caesar's World* and *The World of Columbus and Sons*) offer an informative, narrative, and horizontal approach to world history. Her illustrations and maps make the facts and drama come alive. Of course, sometimes nonfiction and fiction unite, as in David Macaulay's illustrated works of architectural history (such as *Pyramid, Cathedral,* and *Castle*), which combine exquisite line drawings with carefully researched explanations and an engaging fictional narrative.

Fiction, nonfiction, or some combination of both: "living books" are precious, but they are not rare. One final thought: throughout the centuries, God has elected to communicate to his people through the written page. The Bible is the most living of all "living books" (Hebrews 4:12). In it, God presents a wonderful collection of genre—poems and drama, narratives and genealogies, laments and songs. God has placed his stamp on high-quality, idea-rich, stimulating literature. Reading and reading material are special gifts from the Giver of all good gifts. The feast is available. All us, students and teachers, children and parents, need to take and eat!

Picture Study

When Charlotte Mason was on a tour of Florence, Italy, she experienced an epiphany. Impressive frescoes (which we now know were painted by Andrea di Bonaiuta) adorned the walls of the Spanish Chapel in the Church of Santa Maria. Miss Mason would later describe the insights she gained from gazing at those frescoes as the "Great Recognition." The paintings that so captured Miss Mason's heart depict the Holy Spirit's descent as he inspires the minds of men. In di Bonaiuta's frescoes, the apostles, the prophets, and medieval scholar Thomas Aquinas appear in the midst of the divine light of the Spirit, whereas above float figures that represent seven virtues and beneath lie symbols that illustrate fourteen disciplines of academic study. The message of this artistic creation is that when all is first submitted to the divine direction, an absolute harmony exists between education and philosophy. In di Bonaiuta's worldview, spiritual dualism had no validity. Education united not only ideas and activities but also heart and soul.

For Charlotte Mason, the "Great Recognition" was the understanding that God always stands behind valid knowledge acquisition. Every worthy idea ultimately derives from the mind of God. The reason I bring up this anecdote from Miss Mason's life is not, primarily, to reiterate that "all truth is God's truth," nor to decry an education that leaves God out, but rather to highlight how Miss Mason arrived at her epiphany—she studied a picture. From its inception, picture study has stood as a principal piece of a Charlotte Mason education.

Charlotte Mason believed that just as students need firsthand experience with "living books," so too should they develop a personal relationship with great art. Her method was: "Line by line, group by group, by reading, not books, but [by studying the] pictures themselves" (*Philosophy of Education*, p. 214). Miss Mason underscores the importance of the pictures, stating: "As in a worthy book, we leave the author to tell his own tale, so we trust a picture to tell its tale through the medium the artist gave it" (*Philosophy of Education*, p. 214)." Students at Charlotte Mason's school would hear a lot of these artistic tales, for, during their school years, such students were introduced to about thirty artists, absorbing a storehouse of images and learning to distinguish the nuances of many artistic methods and messages.

One of our favorite classroom activities at The Wilberforce School (TWS) is picture study. Over the years, students have discussed works as diverse as those by Edward Hicks and Vincent Van Gogh, N. C. Wyeth and Rembrandt van Rijn, and Giotto and Winslow Homer. As our students examine art prints, they note brush strokes and settings, color and content, light and shape, visual narrative and still life. Picture study is at once simple in method and profound in insight. When students begin a picture study, they sit in silence, appraising a single art print, asking mental questions, and using and stretching their powers of observation. Afterwards, the students take turns sharing their observations and narrating their understandings about the picture's style and significance. A week later, the students return again to the art print. Now the teacher offers information about the life of the artist and the picture's historical and artistic context. Then students are once again encouraged to scrutinize the art print, reflecting on and then narrating the picture in a way that incorporates their newly acquired knowledge.

After students have thoroughly discussed one picture (a process occurring over approximately two weeks), they receive an art print depicting another of this same artist's works. Now the students try both to compare and contrast paintings and to form some initial theories about the artist's unique style and concerns. In the course of a trimester, students will initiate a lifelong acquaintance with this artist as they spend time learning and discussing four or five of his or her works.

Picture study has several benefits. Obviously, it develops the powers of observation, for it trains students to look carefully, closely, and critically. It introduces art history as students come to recognize and discuss schools of art, techniques, and trends. Moreover, since art often reflects cultural, political, philosophical, and economic currents, learning about particular artists teaches about history in general. Picture study also trains students to appreciate the elements of art, which, in turn, makes both art viewing and art creating both more comprehensible and more successful.

Conventional wisdom tells us that "a picture is worth a thousand words." If the thousands of words in "living books" are life transforming—and they are—how much more can a "thousand-word-valuable" painting touch, enlighten, inspire, and please? Each new picture study offers each TWS student a chance for his or her own "Great Recognition." In such cases, picture study and joyful discovery are one and the same.

Music Study

A t The Wilberforce School (TWS), we love music. We daily sing hymns, study about composers and regularly enjoy selections from their works, and frequently discuss the impact of patriotic and historical music on events and people. Because we include so many musical experiences in our regular classrooms, the education that occurs during music class moves beyond music history and appreciation. Instead, TWS students learn about musical performance and composition using a widely known (and primarily vocal) technique known as the "Kodály method."

Named for its Hungarian originator, Zoltan Kodály (1882–1967), this method reflects its author's educational philosophy. According to Kodály, music always must be a core-curricular subject, and correct music study should evidence the following: a belief that anyone capable of lingual literacy is also capable of musical literacy, a recognition that singing is the best foundation for musicianship, and that musical education starts with the very young, an understanding of national folk songs as a musical mother tongue and as such the natural vehicle for early musical instruction, and a commitment that all music taught will be restricted to that of the highest artistic value.

Kodály was more of a facilitator than an originator; in fact, his method eclectically combines John Curwen's tonic sol-fa system and hand signals, Chevé's rhythmic symbols, and Jacques-Dalcroze's *solfège* techniques. For the youngest children, Kodály's musical instruction focused primarily on singing and ear training, ensuring proficiency in those two skills before students moved on to musical notation. In making this choice, Kodály acknowledged the well-known developmental truth that charts the mind's progress from concrete thinking to the more abstract.

Why use the Kodály method at TWS? Basically, we do so because the Kodály method accords so well with our classical/ Charlotte Mason pedagogical approach. This method produces a number of proficiencies that grammar-aged children learn with relative ease and enjoyment. These skills include the ability to differentiate (by ear) major and minor tonality, pitch direction, and volume; the ability to distinguish between no beat, steady beat, and melodic rhythm; and the ability to recognize and name parts of the grand staff, quarter and eighth notes, middle C, treble G, and bass F.

One important part of the Kodály method is group singing. As students learn to sing, play instruments, and dance/ play (all from memory) singing games, chants, and folk songs (both from the students' own heritages and from other cultures and countries), they master musical reading, writing, and part singing. In this way, TWS students learn correct posture and breathing for singing, how to find and sing in their upper registers, and how to use their head voices. All these abilities fit well with the choral performance skills—such as following a conductor (including a conductor's hand signals), enunciating clearly, singing antiphonally, working as a group, and even entering and exiting a stage—which TWS students learn as part of their periodic musical performances that accompany annual school events (such as "Lessons and Carols" in December and "Fine Arts Day" in May).

Although its originator never used this terminology, music instruction, according to the Kodály method, is "a Charlotte Mason" experience. Students delight in listening to, analyzing (using the musical vocabulary they are accumulating through each level of their study), and even performing some of the great music of the world. They also progress from imitation to innovation as they take steps in improvisation and composition. As they grow in their love of music, students simultaneously develop a growing musical literacy.

It has been said, to the point of triteness, that music is the universal language. The Kodály method is designed so that at the same time children are developing physically, socially, emotionally, and spiritually (think Luke 2:40 and Luke 2:52), they are also developing musically (acquiring increasingly complex musical skills and concepts). Of course, no matter how wonderful a program is on paper, it is only as good as its execution. The strength of the music program at TWS lies in how it is taught and how it supports and enhances the community we are creating. We are thankful that from its inception, the TWS music program has offered excellent music instruction in the context of Christian commitment. We never forget that music is God's gift to us, which we return to him through our hymns, praises, and spiritual songs.

CLASSICAL WITH A CHARLOTTE MASON SPIN

Phonics for Reading

One of the cornerstones of The Wilberforce School (TWS) reading program is its phonics instruction, a systematic method that equips our students with the tools to become lifelong readers. Our phonics instruction combines our understanding of the classical emphasis on teaching the grammar of a subject (reading) before its logic and rhetoric and our Charlotte Mason understanding of the primacy of books (and in reading books) in introducing full persons to the world of ideas.

Reading instruction is a subject fraught with controversy. Questions about reading inspire blogs, books, and education schools: Is reading a natural skill, or must it be taught? Should students dissect individual words or just plunge into an entire passage? How much, if any, phonics study is needed? How does an instructor teach for reading fluency? How does a reader move from decoding to critical, discerning reading? While I cannot hope to answer these questions in two short Principia, I can offer a glimpse into the reading instruction at TWS and discuss how it makes use of our grammar-aged students' love of facts and rules.

Phonics instruction is "in." Ask almost any elementary teacher if he or she uses phonics as part of his or her reading lessons, and he or she probably will respond in the affirmative. Be warned, however, that not all that goes by the name of "phonics" is really phonics. In fact, the phrase "phony phonics" has arisen to describe a smattering of inconsistent and frequently random introductions to alphabet sounds and blends. "Phony Phonics" content often encompasses what teachers mean when they proclaim, "We teach phonics." Wanda Sanseri, long-time apologist for Ramona Spaulding's classic phonics text, *The Writing Road to Reading*, shuns not only "phony phonics" but also "pokey phonics" that spreads the teaching of phonogram study over many years and "fickle phonics" that teaches such unreliable rules as "When two vowels go walking, the first one does the talking" (valid only about 25 percent of the time). When speaking to the Oregon Senate (February 2001), Sanseri offered this definition of genuine phonics: "Effective phonics [study] deals with the sounds represented by phonograms and gives a complete, uncluttered, reliable presentation of the code as soon as possible."

Another way to understand phonics programs is to differentiate between implicit and explicit phonics instruction. Most contemporary school classrooms employ only implicit phonics in the teaching of reading. As such, each year classes learn approximately 300 words that are taught as whole words. Students learn how to use context clues, word shape, and beginning and ending letter sounds to distinguish these words. Often paired with whole-language activities in what is termed a "balanced literacy approach," implicit phonics involves whole-to-parts learning.

The method of explicit phonics instruction (an adaptation of Spalding's famous system) at TWS works in the opposite way—from parts to whole. Students learn letters and sounds, phonograms and syllables. As they move systematically through texts that reinforce the phonics skills they are acquiring, these students master the various lettering-sound correspondences. By third grade, students using this explicit approach have mastered the entire code. At that juncture, they can read anything within their comprehension vocabularies, estimated at about 30,000 words rather than a mere 900 sight words (three grades times 300 words).

In more ways than mere word counts, study after study demonstrates the superior efficacy of explicit phonics programs in producing readers who comprehend well and read widely. When coupled with phonemic awareness (the ability to hear the sounds within spoken words), explicit phonics consistently proves to be the most effective method for teaching reading and writing (cf. U.S. Government Printing Office's *Illiteracy in America*).

Despite the proven efficacy of explicit phonics programs, a host of "objections" arise concerning this type of instruction. Criticisms multiply: "We teach higher-order thinking skills, not merely word decoding"; "Phonics instruction is kill and drill"; "Students should learn to read the way they learn to talk—naturally"; "One method cannot work for children when there are so many learning styles." Simple facts reveal these objections as smoke screens. Here are a few brief responses: Studies repeatedly show both that higher-order thinking involves thinking about something and that many times the prerequisite to such thinking is decoding the written text. Phonics instruction, while rote, when undertaken in the grammar stage and presented with creative methodology need not bore. All one has to do is witness our Explorers I students as they jump up and down and announce, "There are phonograms everywhere," to see that these children do not view as tedious their daily phonics instruction.

To see my responses to the other objections to explicit phonics, read on. With regard to "natural reading," the ability to read well is not a guaranteed skill in the way the ability to talk is, a fact illustrated by the high illiteracy rates in many countries. While some people crack the phonetic code on their own and learn to read "naturally," the vast majority of people need systematic instruction in this code. As for learning styles, these differences deal with preferences as to how to learn, not what to learn. Explicit phonics instruction adapts well to all styles of learners; this is why experienced educators routinely choose systematic phonics instruction for teaching reading to dyslexic and even hearing-impaired students. The bottom line is this: Students need to internalize the code that governs written English. Systematic phonics offers early, direct, and intensive instruction in this code. To read well opens a world of insight, pleasure, and information. We dare not fool with a system that works.

TWS chose to teach phonics in a way that highlights the relationship among reading, penmanship, and spelling. Studies have shown that teaching spelling and writing with phonics provides immediate reinforcement of reading skills because students now can write correctly what they are learning to read. Phonics learning at TWS is a relatively easy process. What is so easy, you may ask, about a system that teaches four sounds for the phonogram "o" and six for the phonogram "ough"? This question highlights the developmental difference between an elementary-school child and an adult. For the grammar student, phonograms are easy. By the end of class one, these children can rattle off seventy-two phonograms, play phonogram bingo, list in order six final "e" spelling rules, and tell you when to double the final consonant before adding a suffix.

Systematic phonics instruction is an investment. Time taken early to learn the phonograms, the spelling and coding rules, and the penmanship skills pays off dividends for years in the future. Echoing Aesop's fable of the ant and the grasshopper, the student who works now will play later.

Phonics for Spelling

"My favorite phonogram is <u>ough</u>." "My favorite phonogram is <u>ear</u>, the /er/ of earth, earn, early, learn, heard, search, and pearl" (class one). "To spell the past tense of 'pay' correctly, you have to think about the 'y' part of the phonogram ay" (class four). "If you don't code 'famous" correctly, you end up with 'fame-mouse'. . . now that is funny" (class three). "I love that words have a coding—it's our special secret" (class one). "Knowing phonograms helps me read better" (Explorers II).

In The Wilberforce School (TWS) method of phonics instruction, students move from prereading to decoding to fluency and next to reading to learn (the first steps toward the eventual goal of mature, discerning reading). Our efficient instruction involves a multisensory approach uniting hearing, saying, and writing phonograms (the symbols we use to write the various sounds of our language) with the combining of those mastered phonograms into words and beyond. Students of English have arrived at a finite number of phonograms that comprise our written language (from seventy to ninety-three depending on the number of foreign sounds/spellings included). At TWS, because we follow Ramona Spalding's reworking of the Orton-Gillingham phonogram list, we teach seventy-two phonograms in all.

As TWS students move systematically through texts that reinforce the phonics skills they are acquiring, these students learn and apply the various lettering/sound correspondences. By third grade, our students have mastered the entire phonetic code. At that juncture, they can read anything within their comprehension vocabularies, estimated at about 30,000 words rather than the typical 900 words (often termed "sight" or "high-frequency" words).

Despite this proven efficacy of explicit phonics programs, a host of "objections" arise concerning this type of instruction. One of these criticisms is that phonics study is boring, "death by kill and drill." Phonics instruction, while rote, when undertaken in the grammar stage and presented with creative methodology need not bore. At the beginning of this Principium, a selection of randomly collected quotations from our students belies this nay-saying. Our students love phonograms, whether served up in bees or bingo, the phonogram bus or plane, students as phonogram teachers, or even ordinary chants. They can sing silly phonics songs, proclaim "work" as their middle name, and give the six sounds of "ough" without missing a beat.

Still, phonics instruction at TWS is more than learning seventy-two phonograms and accompanying songs. Were you to glance at the fronts of our students' homework and memory work folders, you would find that these titles are annotated with a series of numbers and lines. While some of these annotations are familiar diacritical marks (such as syllable indicators and the macrons and breves that distinguish long and short vowels), other annotations (such as subscripted and superscripted numbers, slashes, and seemingly random single and double underlines) make little sense to the uninitiated.

After teaching the first fifty-two phonograms, we begin introducing our students to a list of spelling words, the first 100 of which include some of the most common words in English (often called "high-frequency words"). Over the years, TWS students progress through our basic spelling list (about 1,200 words). Relevant spelling rules are introduced as needed, and we apply these rules directly to whatever new vocabulary the students are learning.

Whenever a TWS student is assigned a new spelling word, he or she is led through a process of analyzing and coding that word. The markings used help that student to apply spelling rules and remember the assigned word. Because successful reading and learning from that reading involve noticing and interpreting symbols, the coding process, when taught early in the student's educational career, establishes such scrutiny as habit. The dots, underlinings, and numerals adorning the words are tools for understanding and recalling pertinent information. These labels become hooks for later mental recall, thus enhancing the student's ability both to read and to comprehend what he or she has read. For the younger students at TWS, correct spelling involves correct coding. This extra effort fixes the word in the students' brains, allowing for easier future retrieval and helping to ensure that students will spell the words correctly long after their spelling tests. Eventually, students progress to a point where correct spelling no longer includes coding; still, when students encounter a particularly difficult word, they often revert to coding to help them make the new vocabulary their own.

It is hard for parents to believe, but as time passes, most TWS students genuinely enjoy coding. With relative rapidity, students learn to divide a word into syllables, to analyze each syllable, and to code it with a series of symbols (including, but not limited to, underlines for multiletter phonograms, numbers for the frequency of a sound used, and diagonal slashes for silent letters). For TWS students, coding almost becomes a game as the students try to (and often do) "outcode" their teachers. TWS parents are not even in the competition! Knowing coding makes TWS students initiates of a "special society," one that often baffles the adults (and peers) around them. Thus the task that at first appears to be burdensome becomes the source of satisfaction and of confidence.

Reading Aloud

In Principium 11, I wrote about "living books." Now I want to say that although it is always fine to read a "living book" silently and to one's self, there is also tremendous joy, value, and power in reading aloud in small classroom or family groups.

A glance at The Wilberforce School (TWS) recommended book list is all anyone needs to see that we place a premium on reading aloud. Every class has certain books designated at their yearly "read-alouds." Over the years, I have been fortunate enough to visit classes reading aloud such books as *Aesop's Fables*, Thornton Burgess stories, *Robin Hood, Benjamin Bunny, The Hobbit, Understood Betsy, The Voyage of the Dawn Treader*, and *Star of Light*. While those titles are all fictional works, classroom read-alouds often include biographies of writers such as E. B. White and Beatrix Potter, a number of nature and science books, and Opal Wheeler's discussions of musicians Handel, Mozart, and Tchaikovsky. Obviously, at TWS, we love to read aloud.

Not only is reading aloud great entertainment, but it also is sound educational practice. Repeated studies have demonstrated both that good readers make good students and that the single best way to raise a reader is to read to that child—at school and at home. Why is this true, you might wonder? The answer is: For a number of reasons, beginning with the fact that such children have the value and pleasure of reading modeled to them. Not only do they see that their parents (and teachers) are readers, but they also hear and internalize what reading fluency sounds like and how use of imagination (as demonstrated in such oral techniques as voices and tempo variations) enhances a reading experience.

Reading aloud also teaches students to form mental images (especially when, at least initially, the reader refrains from showing the book's illustrations). A word of caution is due here: When children have problems forming mental images, it is often a result of having spent too much time in front of image-driven television shows, DVDs, and video games. Experiencing the full benefits of reading aloud first may involve the weaning of the listeners from "mental candy," but be encouraged in this task, for listening skills can be developed. Despite the cost, the benefits of reading aloud are worth the effort. Reading aloud also allows students to meet a variety of literary genres, to predict outcomes, to learn vocabulary in context, to hear grammar used correctly and in an enjoyable way, to learn about lives and experiences outside their own, and to build community with the other listeners.

Reading aloud holds a personal meaning for me. I can still remember listening to my great aunts as they read to me, when I was five, from Alcott's *Little Women* (which I mistakenly told someone was "Little Lemon"; I am still not so good on titles). Beth's death always makes me cry! I know, too, that Jean Lee Latham's *This Dear-Bought Land* (about the Jamestown colony), which my fifth grade teacher read to us, introduced me to historical fiction—a favorite genre of mine even today. When an eye operation kept me patched for a week, my mother read out loud *A Portrait of a Lady* (James), from which I could quote extensively three months later when I wrote my college comprehensive exams. No wonder I am such an advocate of reading aloud.

Over the years, a smattering of the great "read-alouds" that I have either read or listened to include *The Sneetches and Other Stories* (Seuss), *The Chronicles of Narnia* (Lewis), *From the Mixed Up Files of Mrs. Basil E. Frankweiler* (Konigsburg), *The Pushcart War* (Merrill), *Watership Down* (Adams), *Farmer Boy* (Wilder), *The Bronze Bow* (Speare), *Our Island Story* (Marshall), *The Landmark History of the American People* (Boorstein), *Carry On, Mr. Bowditch* (Latham), *Robinson Crusoe* (DeFoe), *The Child's History of the World* (Hillyer), *Alice in Wonderland* (Carroll), and *The Child's Story Bible* (Vos). In fact, any "living book" makes a good candidate for a read-aloud.

One fall, my husband and I were asked to suggest favorite children's book titles for an article in a national magazine. Our sons happened to both be visiting, and we laughed as we remembered sharing together the *Trouble with Trumpets* (Wiggins), *Cloudy with a Chance of Meatballs* (Barrett), *Charlotte's Web* (White), *Lyle, Lyle, Crocodile* (Waber), *I Am a Bunny* (Rissom), *Good Night Moon* (Brown), and *Billy and Blaze* (Anderson). While some of these titles may not quite be "living books," all of them were certainly fun reads.

The four of us agreed that reading together played a large part in forging family closeness. Even now, my husband and I will take turns reading books to one another. Don't strive for perfection; enjoy the journey. In our case, there exists the video that my sons pull out all too often, the one that has one son doing everything but listening while I read (and his father tempts him to ham it up for the camera). Nevertheless, reading together sparked conversation, community discussion and discovery, laughter, and learning.

Reading aloud is life-changing. It is much easier to discuss Almanzo's (*Farmer Boy*) or Eustace's (*The Voyage of the Dawn Treader*) disobedience than our own. We can share the danger of hiding a downed American pilot in occupied Holland (*Winged Watchman*) or the thrill of surviving on our own (*My Side of the Mountain*). We can identify with the sacrifices of a true friend (*Charlotte's Web*) or the divided loyalties of border-state living in the Civil War (*Across Five Aprils*).

So many objections to leisure activities fail to apply to reading aloud. Reading aloud is inexpensive. Most communities have free public libraries and an array of worthwhile books. (Challenge your family to read from every different "hundred" of the Dewey Decimal System, as well as from the

F's and B's.) Reading aloud is portable—it is easy to bring a book along to a picnic or a doctor's waiting room. Car drives can be made more palatable by listening together to CDs of a "book on tape." Reading aloud is simple—one does not need any special training or degrees to share a book. I also know (from experience) that a child's time at home passes all too quickly. So I remain passionate with this plea: Read! Read! Read! Reading aloud is a gift to your family that you cannot afford to miss.

Living Lessons from a Dead Language

"*Amo, amas, amat, amamus, amatis, amant*": When visitors walk the halls of The Wilberforce School (TWS), they are likely to hear students conjugating verbs, declining nouns, and discussing the number of spectators that Ancient Rome's Circus Maximus could accommodate. Some very alive students are enjoying and debating Latin, a language too often linked to the quality adjective "dead." Why study Latin anyway, when the chances of meeting a native speaker are so abysmally low?

The answers to the "Why Latin?" question range from the purely pragmatic to the culturally powerful. On the pragmatic side, about half the words in the English language are Latin derivatives, meaning that Latin knowledge, just like phonics study, unlocks our written language. In fact, Latinate words include many of the polysyllabic ones that populate the harder books, so by learning Latin a student acquires a key to greater reading fluency and improved comprehension. In addition, learning any one Latin word exposes a student to a variety of vocabulary. For example, a student may learn that *"frater"* means "brother," so he or she may better understand the English words "fraternal," "fraternity," "fraternize," and even "fratricide." No wonder students of the classical languages (Latin and Greek) consistently score highest on college entrance examinations.

Latin study has other benefits as well. For one, understanding Latin grammar aids students in making sense of the English language. Learning to decline nouns and pronouns helps students to understand both the various roles a noun plays and the differences between subjective and objective cases. At TWS, our Latin and grammar curricula are coordinated. For example, "possessive personal adjective" (PPA) means the same in both language arts and Latin language classes. Latin also helps students to learn additional living languages. Not only do French, Italian, Portuguese, Spanish, and Romanian all derive from Latin, but the principles gleaned from Latin inflection also help students in learning even non-Romance-inflected languages such as German. Finally, although this benefit is years away, some careers—such as law and medicine—make extensive use of Latin terminology.

Of course, when discussing Latin study (especially with a history teacher, as I am), we must acknowledge that the Romans are interesting in and of themselves. They established the first major bureaucratic state based on representative government, and they were a significant Western power for 800 years. Roman law also laid the foundation for most Western legal systems; in fact, "constitution," "citizenship," and "commonwealth" are all Roman terms. When one moves to literature (another of my loves), one discovers that Latin authors prove to be some of the most influential writers in almost any field of the humanities. While we often look back to Greece to understand the Western intellectual tradition, in truth, Greek was essentially forgotten in the West until the Renaissance and did not regain its widespread popularity until the eighteenth century.

It is not possible to talk about Latin without pointing to its long and continuing tradition of literary use. Augustine's Latin writings contributed to the theological development of Christianity. Anselm, Aquinas, Ockham, Erasmus, Calvin, and Spinoza all published primarily in Latin. Even in the case of writers who did not write in Latin, their vernacular output often reflected years of training in Latin. For all the writers of the medieval and early modern period (such as Shakespeare, Racine, Moliere, Jonson, Dante, Chaucer, and Milton), the Latin language and its writers were their primary guides. In the late eighteenth century, Charles Wesley attributed his skill in poetry writing to his training in Latin and Greek. Even today, Caesar's *Gallic War* remains the widest read military memoir (and is still required reading at West Point).

With regard to our philosophical tradition, Latin authors Cicero, Seneca, and Boethius popularized and interpreted Aristotle and Plato. Cicero also greatly influenced Edmund Burke and John Adams, two men whose thoughts still echo in our political system. Latin writers also continue to direct us today because our understanding of logic, argumentation, and rhetoric all derive from Latin expressions of these skills. Knowing the Latin language and reading Latin authors, then, are not merely exercises in cultural literacy but rather are also important steps in understanding our own story.

Latin study is a key component in the accomplishing of TWS' academically rigorous education. Students exercise and develop the habits of thoroughness and attention while speaking, writing, and reading this precise language. They enjoy learning about the life of Ancient Rome and expanding their English vocabulary with Latin derivatives. After having seen and heard TWS students, one is hard-pressed to label Latin as arduous, boring, dull, or irrelevant. At TWS, vibrant young students experience and accept the challenge, power, and joy of discovering how a (supposedly) dead language yet speaks.

Math and Science

G iven the strong emphasis on language-eliciting activities such as narration, dictation, and recitation at The Wilberforce School (TWS), it may be surprising to some observers that we are equally committed to offering robust math and science programs. Any parent who coaches his or her student through nightly TWS math homework or a review of math facts knows the central place mathematics assumes in our studies. At TWS, every class spends approximately an hour on math each day, combining concept instruction with fact drills, mathematical theory, mental math games, and challenge problems. Students do math as part of their daily work sheets, and they review math flashcards and complete daily timed drills. In addition to their daily Saxon math lessons (which run the gamut from operations to measurement, graphing to estimation), students hone their math problem-solving abilities using critical-thinking texts such as *Figure it Out*. During free time, students often employ their mathematical skills by playing one of several math-focused card and board games. On top of all this mathematics activity, students in class four and above train for and take monthly problem-oriented tests as contestants in the nationwide "Math Olympiad" competition.

A word about mathematics curricula: Sadly, there is no perfect curriculum. Each of the best curricula has strengths and weaknesses. On the one hand, Saxon is an excellent curriculum that not only teaches skills sequentially but also continually cycles back in its homework, ensuring that no past skill is forgotten. On the other hand, we at TWS feel compelled to supplement Saxon with additional mathematics theory, fact drills, mental math games, and hands-on modeling. From time to time as well, we read aloud and discuss books that offer the history and philosophy of math and science, such as *Archimedes and the Door to Science* (Bendick). Mathematics is broader than any one curriculum can encompass.

Classical education—one of the main philosophic traditions behind the TWS curriculum—always has placed a premium on both mathematical and scientific education. In addition to training according to the Trivium, classical education introduced experienced young scholars to the Quadrivium, a fourfold technical education encompassing the following: arithmetic, geometry, astronomy (which was broader than the contemporary discipline of the same name), and music. In many interpretations of classical education, the science portion of Quadrivium study is postponed until the students are proficient in the skills that the Trivium reinforces. At TWS, we focus on math and science skills that relate to the grammar and logic stages and leave more complex theory for when students possess the analytical abilities to both interpret and critique that theory. In other words, while we presently emphasize math and science, these disciplines will grow even more essential in rhetoric-aged instruction.

Since we are discussing the Quadrivium, we have now introduced the issue of science instruction at TWS. While some classical schools leave science study to the secondary level, we at TWS follow Charlotte Mason's example of teaching science through nature study beginning in Explorers I. At TWS, nature study focuses on learning and implementing the scientific method—including careful observation and precise data recording, specimen drawing, and research using scientific guides. TWS classes devote regular weekly time to nature study, where students combine handson observation with classroom theorizing and where they link field-guide research and periodic experimentation to drawing and recording in their individual nature journals.

To further illustrate elementary science experimentation, our class one students usually devote a number of weeks to studying about and experimenting with bean plants. As part of their study, students research plant development, make scientific drawings, record data, learn about controls and variables, and in real time seek to understand the ups and downs of plant growth (including dealing with plant pests). Earlier this year, class four students studied scientific classification.

In class four, as part of the study of experimental processes, students learn that nineteenth-century Harvard Professor Louis Agassiz required his students to observe the same fish for hours. Class four's observation specimens were not fish but whole peanuts, which the students studied, drew, described, and finally, retrieved, by making use of their recorded data, from a pile of peanuts.

At TWS, nature study in the early grades is closely linked to life science (particularly botany and zoology). In the middle grades (classes six to eight), we progress through a rotation of physical, earth, and life sciences. While we at TWS agree with the classical educators that detailed data analysis awaits a strong mathematical and statistical understanding, we believe that from the earliest years onward we must model a love of doing science, of asking not only "What?" but also "How?" and "Why?" and of pursuing specific and satisfying answers.

Exercising critical thinking is one key to becoming a good mathematician and a good scientist. The emphasis at TWS on the habits of attention and thoroughness develops scholars who can think about math and science with insight and precision. This is why we teach our students not only how to read but also how to read for meaning and how to read for worldview. We teach them as well that effectual problem solving involves gathering appropriate data, organizing those data in the most useful format (such as chart, list, or scenario), formulating a sensible action plan, and then acting on that plan. We want our students to read science and mathematics as critically as they read history and literature.

When the students enter class six, we add logic study to their daily schedule, again expanding the students' abilities not only to know technical facts but also to make use of those facts in a way that promotes virtue, truth, and beauty. This careful analysis is one activity that distinguishes a classical education from a utilitarian one. Not only do we want our students to know information (such as what we teach them in the fields of math and science), but we also want them to understand how to use that knowledge for the betterment of their world. At TWS, teachers strive to offer a careful balance between empirical observation and academic discipline. Our emphasis on both math and science reflects the order, creativity, and complexity that the Divine Designer placed in his world. We teach our students that factual mastery and careful observation go hand in hand with appreciation, wonder, and discovery.

Hymns of the Month

E ach month at The Wilberforce School (TWS) we learn and sing a "Hymn of the Month." During different times of the day, a careful listener can hear one or another of our classes singing this designated hymn. In addition, as part of the first chapel of each month, I share with students about some aspect of the chosen hymn—its meaning, its history, and/or a biography of its writers (whether the musician or the lyricist). Frequently, parents tell us that they overhear their students singing these monthly hymns while they are at play. Obviously, our children enjoy learning and sharing their monthly hymns. Nevertheless, you may wonder why learning hymns is part of the curriculum at TWS, how we choose our monthly hymns, and what place hymn singing has in contemporary Christian worship.

One of the initial reasons we chose to incorporate hymns into the curriculum at TWS was because many traditional schools, such as those in the Charlotte Mason tradition, encouraged such hymn learning. In Miss Mason's case, one outworking of her clear affirmation of the personhood of children was her desire to lead her students in worshiping their Maker with both knowledge and skill. Such informed worship necessitates not only understanding lyrics but also mastering music. We at TWS also desire that our students participate knowledgeably in worship. We select hymns with theological richness, prompting our students to discuss deep ideas and to learn key concepts. In addition, we try to include hymns that highlight God's creative work (cf. "This is My Father's World"), teach important concepts (such as God's omnipotence in "A Mighty Fortress"), and incorporate seasonal (Christmas—"Angels We Have Heard on High"; Easter—"Crown Him with Many Crowns") and educational themes ("Wilberforce Day"—"Amazing Grace"). In addition, many times the hymns we sing incorporate the very words and themes of Scripture. As our students thought about God's trustworthy Word ("How Firm a Foundation"), they also recalled God's righteous right hand (Isaiah 41:10), his dross-refining work (James 1:8–9), and his abiding presence (Hebews 13:5–6).

Learning hymns exposes our students to elevated language and complex ideas. Our students can define what a "bulwark," a "foe," and a "mortal ill" are. They can talk about words such as "reconciled," "offspring," "incarnate," and "Immanuel." For some of our students, hymn learning also has provided an introduction to metaphor. We have discussed how such concepts as an "imprisoned soul," "nature's night," and "dungeon flamed with light" relate to our own spiritual pilgrimage

("And Can It Be?"). No wonder parents have heard students remark at church, "Look, we're singing my hymn." After over a month of singing and discussion, students come to make these hymns their own.

Another benefit of hymn learning is that it is a stepping stone to understanding both Christian biography and church history. We have learned about Mrs. Cecil Frances Alexander ("All Things Bright and Beautiful"), Isaac Watts ("Joy to the World"), Frances Havergal ("Take My Life and Let It Be"), Charles Wesley ("Christ the Lord Is Risen Today"), and John Newton ("Amazing Grace"). We have talked about the Reformation and the missionary movement, abolition of the slave trade, and the Apostle's Creed. We also have learned exciting stories—how Cecil Frances hid her poems from her stern father, how Martin Luther decided to become a monk after surviving a frightening thunder storm, how John Newton overcame his bitterness after his mother's early death, and how Charles Wesley was able to write an average of ten lines of poetry each day for fifty years. Did you know that John Newton's life includes a great hymn love story, that William Wilberforce's generosity kept Charles Wesley's widow from destitution, or that Martin Luther hid in a "mighty fortress" for an entire year?

As our students progress through TWS, it is our hope that they learn many more church history and hymn stories. Already our students have met abolitionist hymn writer William Cowper (pronounced "Cooper"), a man whose poetic skill inspired that of Wordsworth and Keats. They have learned about the Oxford Movement ("Crown Him with Many Crowns") and about medieval cleric Bernard of Clairvaux ("Jesus the Very Thought of Thee").

In Colossians, Paul enjoins believers to encourage one another with songs, hymns, and spiritual songs. Singing about the wonders of our God should be a daily part of all our lives. Because they are learning only nine hymns a year, TWS students just scratch the surface of the diversity of hymnody open to believers. Of course, families can enjoy hymns apart from school and church hours. Families can follow the example of one TWS family and sing one of "our hymns" as part of family devotions. Another possibility is for a family to take advantage of their student's hymn repertoire and sing together during routine tasks (such as doing chores and even carpooling), thereby transforming responsibility into community building.

Worship music is a gift, an art, and a prayer. Singing hymns anchors our faith in history, in poetry, and in the lives of saints who have come before us. Around the world, church music has served to unite, embolden, communicate, catechize, and praise. It is our prayer that the "Hymns of the Month" at TWS will follow boldly in this tradition.

Words by Heart

Often, as part of special events at The Wilberforce School (TWS), students recite poetry, Scripture verses, or famous prose passages. For "Wilberforce Day," they have recited William Cowper's "The Negro's Complaint"; for "Grandfriends' Day," they have shared Longfellow's "Paul Revere's Ride"; and for "Lessons and Carols," they have presented John 1:1–18. The list goes on. At TWS we recognize the power of memorization as a means of informational and cultural transmission.

Memorization of great texts is one of the key educational tools that we employ at TWS. Mirroring the labors of students in earlier ages, TWS students memorize mathematics facts, the notes of the octave, the names of the continents, the branches of scientific classification, the rules for games, Latin declensions, grammar jingles, and of course, their phonograms. We at TWS reject that early-twentieth-century disparagement of memorization that dismissed this pedagogical method as "kill and drill" and that erected an artificial distinction between memorization and creativity, critical thinking, and comprehension.

This is a misleading, even false dichotomy. Citing research showing memorization as one way for "chunking" and thereby extending working memory capacity, cognitive psychologist Daniel T. Willingham states: "Memory is the residue of thought" (*Why Don't Students Like School*, p. 163). In other words, in addition to being fun and entertaining, memorizing well-chosen verbal content has added benefits. Other brain research confirms that the frequency, intensity, and duration of neurological stimulation are proven keys to brain growth. Not surprisingly, students who devote themselves to the mental discipline of memorization find greater success in other academic areas as well. In addition, studies have found that student scholastic success correlates directly with time devoted to language-rich reading and discussing. Those who learn the words from living poems and routinely share those words with others become better thinkers and scholars.

Stated practically, a student has more time to think creatively about mathematics when he or she does not have to count on his or her fingers to arrive at mathematical answers. A student begins to think critically about history only after he or she has memorized the chronological and geographical pegs that give shape to such thinking. One reason that a student will fail at comprehension is that he or she does not carefully learn the parts from which a whole can be created. Memorization is not the enemy of higher-level thinking but its servant. In fact, many times our mind continues analyzing information (facts) that we have memorized previously, even when we are not consciously aware of this process. "Eureka!" moments often come when we "reflect in tranquility" (from Wordsworth's definition of poetry) on the things that we have seen, experienced, and remembered.

At TWS, we take memorization seriously. We do so because we know that children are sponges, soaking up the many kinds of material they hear, even the material that we wish they would not remember. (The jingles that I can still sing from childhood TV show my age and my wasted youth.) At TWS, we want to fill our students' minds with rich, inspiring, and challenging content. We want to give them material worth ruminating on—the "stuff" not only of repetition but also of meditation.

In addition, we take to heart the biblical admonitions about the priority of carefully feeding one's soul. In Psalm 119, David reminds believers that the way to keep pure is by learning and heeding God's word. As TWS's theme verse (Philippians 4:8) explains, minds grow best by focusing on what is true, pure, lovely, and honorable. Moreover, if, as Jesus so clearly teaches, each of us speaks out of the depths of his or her inner person, we want to provide our students with a profound reservoir of truth, beauty, and goodness from which to draw.

No wonder, when TWS classrooms devote significant time to memorizing, that our faculty carefully selects and balances the passages their students memorize. By helping our students learn the sophisticated verbal patterns of famous poems, speeches, and Bible verses, we take advantage of their God-given desire for language acquisition. So our students intone the rich cadences of the "Gettysburg Address" while learning about the historical context that occasioned those powerful words. They memorize Bible passages that tell about God and our responsibilities in living in right relationship to him and his world. They memorize a variety of poems—some of which offer pithy statements of the habits we want in our lives or others of which are examples of "living" literature, writing that combines artistic quality with a compelling depiction of relevant subject matter.

At TWS, we do not ignore another compelling reason for memorizing poems and passages—memorization strengthens community. Our students like to recall together what they learned last year, and they love to hear a member of a lower grade learning what they term "our poem." Outside the classroom, TWS students have shared their poems with grandparents and toddlers, visitors and nursing-home residents. The feedback we receive is consistent. No matter the venue, our students have met audiences who enjoy a poem or story well told.

Here at TWS we are hooked on memorization—for its efficiency, for its flexibility, for its pleasure, and for its cognitive, affective, and spiritual benefits. Words learned by heart are often words that form and shape a heart. In verse and prose, our students have felt the slave's plight, have rehearsed the activities of love, have learned the virtue of perseverance, have relived the Christmas story, have pondered history's exigencies, have gained new language to discuss trees and pilgrims and seasons and weather, and have shared experiences of hymn writers through the centuries. Everyday memorization opens new worlds to our students. Their growth and success underscore this truism: A God-given mind and a God-sensitive heart are both a shame to waste.

Sharing Words from the Heart

In The Wilberforce School (TWS) curriculum, memorizing and recitation operate together, serving and reinforcing each other. So this explanation naturally follows the insights offered in Principium 20. At TWS, a student or group of students demonstrates what has been memorized through recitation. In fact, because a class's goal is so often recitation and not merely individual knowledge acquisition, the simple memorizing of a poem or passage amounts to only the first half of the class's assignment. Only when a student knows the words of a poem is he or she ready to begin tackling the intricacies of group recitation. Good unison recitation is a talent that involves understanding the memorized piece, comprehending recitation methodology, and then taking time (sometimes a lot of time) to practice, practice, and practice some more. There are a number of skills that must unite if a piece of rote memory can be transformed into a pleasing recitation.

After memorizing the words of the poem or passage, students then must work on vocal and visual presentation. The vocal aspects of recitation are complex and include enunciation, dynamics, tone, rhythm, projection, and inflection. The children learn to speak loudly and clearly, but without shouting. They learn that good recitation must occur at a moderate pace so that the group's words sound neither plodding nor choppy. Beyond this, students train their voices to match the mood of the piece, and they also work hard to create and maintain a clear volume.

As a matter of fact, the voice is only one of the "instruments" that the reciting class must manipulate. Students also have to control and exploit the physical communication that comes from posture, stance, and gesture. Just as the children's voices are in unison, so the children's movements occur together. If hand motions are added to the recitation, students must coordinate these gestures precisely as well. All TWS presenters learn to stand straight and tall and, unless otherwise directed, to keep their hands at their sides. Any desired hand or body motions are to be performed by the group as a whole; individual motions distract from the recitation. What is not there is as important as what is carefully added. Slouching can distort a child's tone, make projection difficult, and distract from the overall visual presentation. Twisting motions, unnecessary hand gestures, or head nods can prevent the audience from being able to concentrate on the passage being presented. A proper posture with calculated gestures makes a recited poem memorable. Effective recitation carefully combines the two God-given communication languages—vocal and body language.

Why take all this time in the schedule at TWS to perfect our recitations? We do so because of the many benefits that accrue from recitation activities. When students recite what they have learned, they pay more attention to the words and concepts because they combine their task with the intent to remember. Moreover, for some children, only when they hear themselves saying material aloud do they really learn it. All students benefit from the immediate teacher feedback that accompanies classroom recitation. Students who recite and receive feedback are likely to learn material correctly and to avoid misunderstandings and inaccuracies. Brain research tells us that hearing and reciting involve different parts of the brain and that the more senses we use, the stronger the neural trace we establish. Because recitation allows students to entertain others, to use their dramatic abilities, and to see the results of their hard work and teamwork, its importance is triply underscored.

Parents can help their students to work toward skilled recitation. When a student practices his or her recitation at home, parents can share with him or her that the goal is not memorization, but presentation. Presents given at birthdays or special occasions usually are wrapped carefully and brightly not only to show the care that went into choosing the gift but also to demonstrate that the giver values the person receiving the gift. Thus *presenta*tion is part of the present. Parents can remind their students that their gifts of memorized verse and

Scripture should be wrapped "in the bright papers of thoughtful presentation" so that the recitation will be received with the greatest joy. Parents should applaud their students' progress and encourage their delights also. As a student improves his or her memorization skills, he or she may discover that it truly is better to give than to receive. In addition, a carefully practiced recitation is a gift that one can keep on giving, for a well-learned passage can remain in one's mind, ready to be shared with others, for years to come.

EDUCATING
FOR ETERNITY

Communicating a Biblical Worldview

Every year at The Wilberforce School (TWS) we spend time evaluating—remembering, refocusing, and improving. To do so, we always review our school's mission and philosophy and ask ourselves if we are accomplishing what we set out to do. One of our objectives as listed under our goal of "providing a distinctively Christian education" is that the rich curriculum we teach would communicate an orthodox, biblical view of the world. Christian worldview instruction underlies all we do at TWS.

Perhaps some perspective would help. In 2001, George Barna published his findings about teenagers and spirituality. He discovered that most Christian young people were unable to communicate their faith in a serious, articulate, and confident manner. Barna asked his readers: "What are you doing to enable young people to understand the notion of moral truth, the idea of absolutism in a culture of relativism, and to commit to developing a biblical worldview that is founded on God's unchanging truth?" (*Real Teens*, p. 159). Later, Barna returned again to the worldview issue, arguing that worldview training must begin in children's earliest years. In *Transforming Children into Spiritual Champions*, Barna wonders: "Who will promote the single most important set of skills they [children] need to succeed according to God's standards—their moral and spiritual bearings?" (pp. 47–48). These pointed questions underscore the need for Christian parents and teachers who will instruct the next generation in the components and expressions of a comprehensive and coherent worldview. Christian children need both a "way to look" at the world and a "way to live" in that world. We in Christ's body must equip our sons and daughters so that they may continue, unbroken, the perpetual relay of truth.

What, then, are the basics of this worldview that we seek to pass on in our day-to-day instruction at TWS? What sets of assumptions correctly describe the makeup of our world? What truths not only explain and interpret reality but also translate into real-life experience? To answer these questions, we must consider worldviews in general. Fully formed worldviews answer these four summary questions:

1. Where are we? (In what type of a prime reality do we find ourselves?)

2. Who are we? (What is humanity in both substance and destiny?)

3. What is wrong with where we are and who we are? (In what ways, and why, does this world deviate from its created nature?)

4. How can these wrongs be remedied? (How can this world and its inhabitants be restored to their created purposes?)

At TWS, we are intentional both about teaching God's answers to these four questions and about living out our creed. We long that our students understand the true narrative of who they are and where they live so that they will walk in a way that brings glory to God. Every day, in various ways, we discuss and incarnate these answers to the four worldview questions:

1. Where are we? We live in a world created by the great and good trinitarian God, who is moral compass, definer, and governor of created existence.

2. Who are we? As human beings, we are image-bearers of this trinitarian God, and our hearts reveal our understandings of life and reality.

3. What is wrong both with our "where" and with us? A catastrophic fall has affected human hearts and minds, producing both personal idolatries and spiritual warfare. In addition, this fall has skewed our understandings of reality and the meaning of life.

4. How can these wrongs be remedied? In Jesus Christ, the kingdom of God has altered human history, so our

Savior has both atoned for sin and defeated hostile spiritual forces. The ultimate result of this victory will be restoration of creation to its original purposes.

How do we at TWS communicate such grand truths to young minds? We use an array of methods. We read about these truths—in the Bible, in our living literature books, in history. Sometimes our focus is on what happens when these truths are spurned. Thus we note the dire results when Ahab, King Saul, and Sapphira defy God's standards. Each new event and story we measure against God's standards and desires. From this vantage point, we recognize ethnic prejudice in *Sign of the Beaver*, selfish pride in *Johnny Tremain*, and sacrifice in *Charlotte's Web*. In history class, we uncover both the bravery and the pettiness of American colonists, the daring of Lewis and Clark, and the horrors of chattel slavery.

Reading becomes a springboard to discussion of worldview—as part of daily narrations, chapel messages, and literature, picture, and composer study. Poems such as "The Negro's Complaint," "It Can Be Done," and "The Midnight Ride of Paul Revere" spark conversations on justice, determination, and courage. Memorizing Scriptures such as Psalms 8 and 24 tells us about who we are and whom we serve. The interactions of daily school life—at assembly and playtime, at Latin and gym classes—provide a myriad of opportunities to live out our convictions. We learn to welcome each other, valuing the personhood of each member of our community. We work on preferring others over ourselves, for example, handing the ball to someone who has not had a turn even if our team does not score a point. We seek to encourage and edify each other with our talk, to celebrate others' successes, and to comfort those who feel loss. Our focused attempts to develop habits of obedience, attention, courtesy, and kindness are not so that we can earn merit but so that we can reflect and herald God's grace and goodness.

We at TWS are interested in equipping our students to influence their world as they use their varied talents in the service of Christ's kingdom. We know that acquiring a biblical worldview is fundamental to influencing the world for God and his truth. We long for our students to develop serious, articulate, and confident personal faiths that will attract people from many worldviews to the God of truth. Because we truly want to see our children become spiritual champions, we place a premium on worldview instruction and its practical daily application.

Growing Christian Community

Ever since the inception of The Wilberforce School (TWS), two main avenues of Christian communal life have characterized our school: daily Bible reading and weekly chapel services. Daily, for periods from fifteen to forty-five minutes (shorter in the lower-school and longer in the middle-school years), each class at TWS meets as a group to read and discuss the Bible. At TWS, we follow a program that allows us to read through the Bible every four years (of school days). As part of their students' "life's work," TWS families also are encouraged to follow this same Bible reading program—taking time at home to read and discuss the daily passage. In this way, students receive two passes through the day's text and thus can continue and expand their new biblical understandings in the context of their homes.

As for Bible versions, our youngest students read from Catherine Vos's *Story of the Bible*, whereas class two and above read directly from an actual Bible translation (at school, the English Standard Version). Bible reading is not the same as Bible class; Bible reading is more informal and less prescribed. It offers a chance to peruse a passage, to narrate it, and as time permits, to discuss issues and ideas that surface. TWS classrooms have concordances and other Bible reference tools at hand so that students can practice finding answers to their scriptural questions.

The benefits of systematic Bible reading are many. We hope that our students will develop lifelong habits of daily Bible reading and application. Also, those who stay at TWS for ten years will have the privilege of more than two (more than four if they repeat the readings at home) trips through the Bible. What a rich spiritual and intellectual resource to build a life on! In addition, the fact that all of us at TWS are reading the same Bible passages provides a tremendous unifying force to our school—different members of the community at TWS can allude to our reading at various times during the day or at our weekly chapels. Moreover, because TWS classes (before or after Bible reading) often share prayer requests and then pray together, Scripture reading is part of a pattern of reciprocal caring. Thus, on top of the blessings inherent in reading and heeding God's Word, we at TWS have the honor of mutual prayer based on the promises of this same Word. This daily practice of hearing from and speaking to our Lord is sheer privilege; we do not take it for granted.

While we at TWS believe that an attitude of worship should inform all of life—lessons and playtime, service and artistic expression, assemblies and quiet moments, Friday chapels are the chief method for the community at TWS to experience large-group united worship. Each week, students, faculty, visitors, and staff come together to sing, to pray and to learn how to integrate head and heart knowledge concerning God and his will. As we share hymns, listen to and interact with our speakers, and enjoy each other's company, we discover new ways to respect our God, to grow more like him, and to praise his name.

At TWS, the faculty models a reverent approach to chapel. Chapel is a serious time for our students, one in which they are held to a high standard of behavior and attitude. Their love and consideration for their fellow students require that they reign in desires to wiggle, distract, chat, and entertain. During TWS chapel, both individuals and the group act differently from the norm. Our school shuts down (as it were), allowing everyone to join together and visibly demonstrate how essential chapel is to our educational life. For all of us at TWS, fully engaged chapel attendance is a gift to our fellow believers; we want to encourage, edify, and participate with them.

Chapel offers both immediate and long-term advantages. One purpose of chapel is to prepare future church leaders. By modeling group prayer, congregation singing (of an array of songs and hymns derived from many eras in church history), and the role of the Scriptures in uncovering both theological and life principles, we hope that our students will see patterns they can both emulate and promulgate for years to come. We also encourage our students to serve in the chapels by answering questions that our various speakers pose, by acting in role-plays and demonstrations, or by sharing recitation and musical skills.

No TWS chapel is exactly alike. Just this year we have hosted a multiplicity of speakers (seven different) and considered a variety of topics. This is not to say that we have a haphazard approach to chapel. On the first Friday of a new month, we devote ourselves to learning about the "Hymn of the Month"—its writers (lyricists and musicians), its context, and its meaning. Most other weeks each month, chapel messages have offered a systematic discussion of the year's focus—such topics as the Apostle's Creed, the Lord's Prayer, and the Bible passages of the week. Periodically throughout the school year, TWS offers special chapels. On these special days, we offer a biblical look at the concepts that the particular day highlights. So we may talk about hearts on "Grandparents' Day" (in conjunction with student presentations of words we have learned "by heart") and about the incarnation at our Christmastime service of "Lessons and Carols."

One special aspect of Friday chapels is that they are open to all TWS families. Every week we have guests come and share our time of worship. It is a delight each week for different students to host their parents, other relatives, and special friends. Neither Bible reading nor Friday chapel is a mere appendage to the experience at TWS. These activities are, instead, points of integration—times when we affirm that our school is not merely a temporal institution but a place of mission and of calling.

Educating Purposefully

Already I have shared with you twenty-four essays, a potpourri covering such diverse topics as education, discipline, recitation, mathematics study, and phonics. Fueling all these Principia is the determination at The Wilberforce School (TWS) to think deeply and critically about each aspect of education and, having done so, to act purposefully in applying our mission and philosophy to daily classroom life. Why are we so thorough, so decidedly methodical in analyzing—and then articulating—not only what we are doing but also why we are doing it? Chiefly because we know we are accountable—to God, to our students, to their parents, and to our support community.

In the book of James (3:1), the writer exhorts his readers not to all be teachers because teachers have twice the responsibility—they are accountable not only for their own lives but also for the lives of their students. We who teach at

TWS know that our students are a trust from the living God, and it is to him we stand accountable for the way we help these students to develop not only mentally and physically but also spiritually, socially, and emotionally. As delegated representatives of our students' parents, we are accountable to them as well, reinforcing the values and priorities of their Christian homes. These parents have entrusted their students to us so that we can nurture thinkers who evince the moral and educational habits that will promote success both in school and in life.

We at TWS are accountable not only for the lives God has entrusted to us but also for the vision he has given us, a vision that unites a broad view and a quotidian aspect. While we are seeking to equip our students for eternity, we are doing so in the realm of the day-to-day experience of the class-room. So it is with philosophical gravity that we approach our educational task—whether the focus is the entire school year or the rhythm of a single day. To illustrate this point, I will spend the rest of this essay considering how the vision of TWS reveals itself in one annual ("Reading Rally") and one daily (morning recess) activity.

Every February, TWS sponsors its annual "Reading Rally." For those of us living in the Northeast, February can be a dark and dreary month. For TWS students, however, it becomes a month full of adventure, discovery, and friendly competition. As its mission and philosophy statement clearly underscores, TWS offers a "reading-rich" learning environment—a place where students develop a love of books, especially works of enduring beauty. While we add an element of competition to the "Reading Rally," our focus throughout is on honing reading skills in the context of a growing love for literature. We know that we are succeeding not only because our students achieve their challenge reading goals but also because of the feedback we receive. For example, one of our teachers overheard a class three student remarking to her friend: "This is a good book. I brought a copy for you to read." We love parental reports that our students are reading voraciously, discussing (and even debating) which books to add to our library, and discovering new literary genre. Recognizing a responsibility to steward both minds and hearts, the vision of TWS includes both measurable (to build a great library) and more abstract (to promote lifelong reading among our students) goals. The "Reading Rally" is an important step in promoting this balanced vision.

Since life is so often a succession of "little things," we at TWS are concerned not only about our yearly calendar but also about our daily one. Every morning our classes have a midmorning break. During these times, students eat snacks and have free time, both of which, weather permitting, occur outdoors. This means that our break also includes putting on and taking off sneakers, grabbing water from the cooler, and using the facilities. It is an active, productive interval.

Some people might question the value of playtime, dismissing it as a seeming frill in the day's educational calendar and arguing that the time could be devoted to further academic endeavors. We at TWS disagree. We are so scrupulous about maintaining this midmorning break both because of the needs of our students and because of the educational value of playtime. Visitors to our school have remarked that our days have little "fluff." That is an understatement. From assembly on, classes are busy—daily work, recitation, Bible reading, homework corrections, phonics review, math meetings, reading comprehension, spelling, and vocabulary work are just a sampling of those first two hours at TWS. Following Charlotte Mason's precept of short lessons, we at TWS accomplish a lot quickly, but by 10:30 our students need to exercise their larger muscles (and calm their growling stomachs).

Playtime allows time to, literally, "run off steam." It also offers opportunities for creative problem solving, relationship building, sportsmanship learning, and memory making. Playtime at TWS is chaperoned but not programmed. Our students have space to run, and balls, ropes, and chalk (as well as colored pinnies and cones) with which to play. Still, they are free to organize group games, such as capture the flag (with teachers as willing referees), four-square, or hopscotch. Students also may just talk, pretend they are horses or Rocky Mountain explorers, observe the natural world, or play a board game. Choice of activities often necessitates negotiation, planning, and recruiting of teammates.

Once the games begin, TWS students learn both the joy of victory and the agony of defeat, how to encourage the faint-hearted, and how to win with humility. Playtime becomes a laboratory for the maturing of important life skills, such as working with people of different ages. TWS teachers adopt a balanced approach to playtime supervision. While we want our students to use their own ideas and initiative, we will step in (when necessary) to ensure safety, kindness, and somewhat equal teams. As always, we are also available to help our students grow in wisdom, compassion, and perspective as they work through unavoidable conflicts with each other and, at times, even with their referees.

The book of Proverbs reiterates the importance of planning. Translating Solomon's admonition "to know well your flocks" into our era and situation, we at TWS seek to know well our students, our curriculum, and our community. The willingness to continue to ask what motivates our choice of activities reflects a commitment to keep our vision central. We understand that the decisions we make have long-term effects. Solomon's admonition about personal hearts can be extended to the heart of a Christian organization: "Keep your heart with all vigilance, for from it flow the springs of life" (Proverbs 4:23).

Epilogue: Begin with the End in View

As the subtitle of this book makes clear, no succinct descriptor captures the educational philosophy behind The Wilberforce School. I am well aware of the fact that describing our special education is no easy task. It is my hope that these twenty-four essays have clarified what we mean when we describe ourselves as "a classical Christian school with a Charlotte Mason influence." One way we have developed to capture The Wilberforce Scvhool is with a four-word image: We are "making modern-day Daniels." In this final essay, I would like to camp on this metaphor for a bit and ponder various implications of this powerful ideal.

Daniel was, of course, an Old Testament prophet who lived in turbulent years spanning the Neo-Babylonian captivity of Israel through the Persian conquest. In 606 bc, Daniel, along with a select group of Israelite youths, joined the first wave of Israelite captives when he was abducted and sent to the Babylonian court to be trained as a leader of an anticipated captive Israelite nation. The Book of Daniel not only records the prophet's captivity but also presents and explains his various visions and recounts his miraculous stay in a lion's den. From his youth, when he refused to eat polluted foods, through his middle years, when he confronted gluttonous, irreverent Belshazzar, to his maturity, when he worked as a Persian *satrap* and prayed regularly even in the face of death, Daniel lived out his faith practically, boldly, and decisively.

The modern-day Daniel that TWS seeks to produce is a person who lives out a single-minded Christian faith. This is why a biblical worldview pervades our curriculum. Only those who know God's word will know his will, and only those who know his will are able to represent him in a secular, sensual, and often hostile environment. At TWS, we read and discuss the Scriptures so that we understand who we are and what our calling is. Our biblical-worldview emphasis is not just a devotional time experience; it is an everyday outlook that informs our approaches to literature, history, art, nature, and music. Even during his teenage years, Daniel lived faithfully in a venue where both his superiors and his neighbors rejected his view of God, beliefs, and values. We want to bathe our students in God's truth, encouraging them to apply it to their daily challenges, disappointments, and triumphs so that, when confronting the allurements of a too-often defiling and debasing world, they too will stand apart as champions for their Lord and for his kingdom.

When Daniel (and his friends) was taken captive, he was chosen because he fit the Babylonian want ad: "[Bring] people of the royal family, of the nobility, youths without blemish, of good appearance and skillful in all wisdom, endowed with knowledge, understanding, learning and competent to stand in the king's palace and. . . [to learn] the literature and language of the Chaldeans" (Daniel 1:4).

In other words, these teens were quality specimens, chosen to receive and profit from an academically rigorous education. Daniel 1:17 and 20, however, tells us that these youth's subsequent academic success resulted not merely from raw talent but also from a god-fearing lifestyle: "God gave them [Daniel and his three friends] learning and skill in all literature and wisdom. . . . in every matter of wisdom and understanding about which the king inquired of them, he found them ten times better than all the magicians and enchanters. . . in all his kingdom."

One of the reasons, we at TWS promote classical methodology such as recitation, dictation, and Latin study is that our students thrive amid this rigor. Schooled in the age-old Trivium, TWS students learn to grasp the grammar, logic, and rhetoric of various disciplines. They "gobble up" Chester math drills, musical notation, and Dettmer coding. But TWS is not about stuffing heads with knowledge and hearts with pride. We teach the Trivium as a pattern of knowledge, understanding, and wisdom that is best evidenced in Christ, who uniquely is "The Way, the Truth, and the Life."

Chronology assures us that Daniel could not have experienced an education infused with a "Charlotte Mason influence," although the Book of Daniel certainly talks about art (such as a mammoth statute, 3:1), music (an array of instruments is described, 3:5), and nature (Daniel 4 and 7). As for habits, Daniel was quite accomplished at attending to the details of a dream and then accurately narrating back those details and, of course, interpreting them. He also had some well-defined personal habits, such as a prayer life that led him to meet ("up close and personal") both lions and the Archangel Michael (Daniel 6 and 10). What is obvious in all Daniel's actions is that he knew how to listen to and obey his God, how to persevere in trials and how to maintain his integrity in the face of variegated opposition (fickle kings, jealous fellow workers, unholy rites, nonkosher foods, etc.). Certainly Daniel had laid down "the rails of habit" 2,000 years before the railroad era was conceived.

A truism for reaching a specific goal successfully is to know what that goal is. The maxims proclaiming this viewpoint are both many and clichéd: "Begin with the end in view." "Aim at nothing, and you hit it every time." "It is a dream until you write it down; then it is a goal." Teachers and parents know that the way our children "end up" depends, in part, on what our goal has been and how that goal has informed the journey toward that "end." Someone has said that goals are dreams with deadlines. When teaching children, one must remain acutely aware of deadlines. The days and years will pass quickly; young scholars grow up. Those of us who choose the "joyful rigor" pedagogy do so with a God-inspired hope, prayer, and trust that he will use our all-too-flawed efforts to forge "modern-day Daniels," men and women who will serve him wholly, creatively, and compassionately in their generation.

Suggested Reading List

A number of excellent resources exist that explain and exemplify the specifics of classical Christian and Charlotte Mason education. Below find a *very* abbreviated list of suggested readings to guide study of this topic.

Andreola, Karen. *The Charlotte Mason Companion.* Quarryville, PA: Charlotte Mason Research and Supply Co., 1998. *For almost thirty years, Karen Andreola, along with her husband Dean, has both implemented and written about Charlotte Mason's educational system. The Andreolas are responsible for reissuing Miss Mason's six-volume educational series described elsewhere in these suggested readings. Especially helpful are Andreola's writings on narration and nature study. Her book,* Pocketful of Pinecones *(2001), illustrates and explains nature journaling.*

Bluehorn, Harvey, and Laurie Bluehorn. *Teaching the Trivium: Christian Homeschooling in a Classical Style.* New Boston, IL: Trivium Pursuit, 2001. *Long-time classical homeschoolers, the Bluehorns explain many aspects of classical education while underscoring the biblical Trivium of knowledge, understanding, and wisdom. Their book offers suggestions for teaching at all levels of the Trivium, experience gained through real-life experiences. The Bluehorns also have produced logic textbooks that are entertaining and informative.*

Cholmondeley, Essex. *The Story of Charlotte Mason.* Petersfield, UK: Child Light, 2000. *Essex Cholmondeley knew Charlotte Mason well. (The work was published originally by Dent in 1960.) In this volume, Cholmondeley combines a biography of Charlotte Mason with samplings of her writings. This is an excellent volume both for clarifying facts about Miss Mason's life and for offering provocative Mason writings to narrate and discuss.*

Cooper, Elaine, ed. *When Children Love to Learn: A Practical Application of Charlotte Mason Philosophy for Today.* Wheaton, IL: Crossway Books, 2004. *This book provides an excellent introduction not only to Miss Mason's philosophy but also to its implementation in the classroom. Readers should note that at times a completely "Mason school" will differ from a classical school with a "Mason influence." Have fun looking for the differences!*

King, Jenny. *Charlotte Mason Reviewed: A Philosophy of Education.* Petersfield, UK: Child Light, 2000. *While reading Charlotte Mason is best, for those that want an overview of her thinking without making a large time commitment, this book offers a clear, concise summary of Charlotte Mason's educational system. Read this book for an introduction or as a means to clarify your gleanings from other Charlotte Mason writings. Don't allow it to substitute for reading Charlotte in the originals, but use this piece as an inspiration for further Charlotte Mason reading.*

Macaulay, Susan Schaeffer. *For the Children's Sake.* Wheaton, IL: Crossways, 1984. *With this book, Macaulay helped to* popularize the Charlotte Mason method in America. After participating in a Charlotte Mason school in England, Schaeffer was eager to spread the vision "across the pond." Her sequel, For the Family's Sake, applies Miss Mason's principles to home life.

Mason, Charlotte. *Philosophy of Education*. Wheaton, IL: Tyndale House Publishers, 1989. *Each of Miss Mason's six volumes (jointly entitled,* The Original Home Schooling Series) *is worth reading, but this final volume provides a cogent explanation of her educational thought. Her* Home Education *focuses on schooling before age seven, and* School Education *looks at the years from seven to fourteen.* Parents and Children *is a collection of the teachings on the vital role that parents have in building their children's character and reinforcing habits that will make life's challenges easier. Both* Ourselves *and* Formation of Character *offer stories illustrating Miss Mason's "habits" for study and life; as such, these volumes could serve as the basis for family reading and discussion.*

Pearcey, Nancy. *Total Truth: Liberating Christianity from its Cultural Captivity*. Wheaton, IL: Crossways, 2005. *Does the idea of developing a biblical worldview seem daunting? Nancy Pearcey explains the "creation, fall, and redemption" paradigm—examining it in relation to a wide spectrum of worldviews. Pearcey argues against a sacred-secular divide—advocating instead a holistic approach, one that reflects a personal commitment to "total truth."*

Sayers, Dorothy L. "The Lost Tools of Learning." Essay available online at HYPERLINK *"http://www.gbt.org/text / sayers.html" www.gbt.org/text/sayers.html. Sayers' wellargued* defense of the *Trivium* provoked a return to classical education in the late twentieth century. *Read it and note how Sayers applies her developmental understanding of the trivium to the intellectual lives of children.*

Sockey, Jenny. *For the Love of Learning.* Fairfax, VA: Xulon Press, 2002. *Sockey provides a book list for those who want to find twaddle-free reading. Sockey is a former homeschooler; in her own home teaching, she sought to unite classical, Christian, and Charlotte Mason ideas.*

Wilson, Douglas, with Marvin Olasky. *Recovering the Lost Tools of Learning: An Approach to Distinctly Christian Education.* Wheaton. IL: Crossway Books, 1991. *This book articulates the rationale behind the modern classical Christian school movement. A founder of the Logos School (Moscow, ID) and ACCS, Wilson writes passionately about the need for Christian education as opposed to that offered by "government schools."*

Wise, Jessie, and Susan Wise Bauer. *The Well-Trained Mind.* New York: W.W. Norton and Company, 1999. *Jessie Wise and Susan Wise Bauer (mother and adult daughter) write about their own experience gained from years of classical homeschooling. They also provide guidelines, curricula, and booklists for anyone who would want to educate classically, whether at home or at school. Since readers of this book often bemoan their missed years of classical education, Susan Wise Bauer also has written a self-study program entitled,* The Well-Educated Mind: A Guide to the Classical Education You Never Had.

THE MISSION IN THE
UPPER SCHOOL

Introduction to Three
Additional Chapters

Over ten years have passed since *Joyful Rigor*'s publication; not surprisingly, The Wilberforce School has changed. The students pictured on the cover of that first edition are now scattered to various colleges! Beyond that, our school location has changed three times, while our facilities, faculty, and student body have tripled. Also, in the fall of 2014, we opted to add an Upper School to what had been a JK-Grade 8 school. With that expansion, we unleashed an array of new courses, activities, challenges, and adventures.

Still, The Wilberforce School has not changed its fundamentals: the school remains dedicated to embracing classical Christian education in an atmosphere of discovery and joy. Older students have led us into national debate competitions and created a cappella groups, applied MATLAB programming and judged House Tournaments, and taken mission trips and written college application essays. They have done so as part of our missional commitment to develop "a community of learners engaged in the rigorous exploration of reality, the free and disciplined exchange of ideas, and active participation in the fine arts."

To describe what "Joyful Rigor" looks like at the Upper School, I decided to add three more chapters to this second edition of the book. In so doing, I will answer these questions:

1. *How does The Wilberforce School's philosophy of education enrich and direct the Upper School experience?*

2. *At The Wilberforce School, what pedagogical distinctives characterize these four rhetoric years, and why have you made certain non-traditional choices for your students and their scholastic experience?*

3. *Why is The Wilberforce Upper School more interested in process than product, and how does this process emphasis actually produce better lifelong "products"?*

As I answer these questions, I will provide various glimpses into The Wilberforce Upper School experience. I hope that you see how these final four years capitalize upon and complete the education begun all the way back in Junior Kindergarten. Trained in the habits of life and study that make for virtuous scholarship and discerning service, Wilberforce students can be not merely lifelong learners but also lifelong servants, believers whom God can use both in the wise care and governance of His creation and in the building of His kingdom.

Why an Upper School?

Having an Upper School had never been our plan. From its inception, The Wilberforce School was modeled after a JK–8 school. Our curriculum fit that model, and we happily grew (one grade per year, from our 2005 JK–3 student body to JK–8 by 2010). Then, for four years, we happily sent our Grade 8 graduates on to private and public high schools. And we breathed a sigh of relief. Without Grades 9 through 12, we did not have to worry about college—whether college-prep courses, college entrance examinations, college applications, or college choices. Also, middle school sports, clubs, and community concerns seemed smaller and less exhausting than their high school counterparts. But then facts stood in the way: our student population always aged. The same children that caused us to consider a JK–8 Christian school were now completing their Wilberforce years.

Soon the decision to add an Upper School to The Wilberforce School reflected the similar hopefulness and concern to that which had inspired our 2005 beginnings. Our missional commitments had not changed; we wanted to complete the distinctively Christian, academically excellent, classical, and joyful education we had begun. To do so meant we needed to prepare teachers and adopt texts fitted to the specific needs of rhetoric-aged (roughly age 14 and above) students. We wanted our high schoolers to reflect, discuss, create, think, and serve in a community characterized by truth, goodness, and beauty. We had a big task.

What made the task of adding an Upper School surmountable were two wonderful providences. One, we had lost our lease in what we intended to be our long-term location, and our newly found rental home had enough space to add a fledgling Upper School. Two, we discovered a high school curriculum that complemented what we were already doing, and so began our partnership with Trinity Schools, Inc., (headquartered in South Bend, IN). Space, curricula, mentors, and goals—we had the elements for our new adventure. Now we needed to communicate our new "why" to our community (parents and teachers alike). We needed to embrace our vision for Upper School teachers, texts, and students.

Study after study explaining educational success concludes that, outside of the role of parents, the key determinant of student success is the teacher. All of a sudden, The Wilberforce School needed a new collection of teachers— ones who not only knew their subject and how to translate it to the high school-aged student, but who were also adept at classical pedagogy, including close reading of texts, Socratic discussion, and analytical essay writing. In addition, we needed teachers to instruct our students in college-level modern languages (Spanish and Mandarin) and STEM subjects that included Multivariable Calculus and MATLAB. Our administration bought ourselves a little time by only opening our 2014–15 Upper School to students in Grades 9 and 10, following Trinity's advice that their curricula goals were rarely "obtainable" when students tried to jump into their schools during Junior or Senior years.

At The Wilberforce School, we already had a strong faculty, and we soon gained others—a veteran teacher from a local preparatory school, a Humane Letters teacher from one of Trinity's sister schools, plus Middle School teachers who were fully equipped to teach at a higher level. But after years of saying we were happy to stop with eighth grade, we still had to translate our amended "why" into language our faculty could understand and embrace. The answer lay in the purpose of our education. Named after abolitionist and reformer William Wilberforce, our school had always emphasized responsibility to others by means of active service and the stewardship of gifts and opportunities. William Wilberforce learned, as his biographer John Pollock says, that he could change the world, but he could not do it alone. Like Wilberforce, our graduates would need to not only embrace vigorous academic conversation but also to do so in a way that incorporated a community of difference-making persons also committed to transforming their world.

These were high ideals for thirteen-year-olds; they are high ideals for eighteen-year-olds as well. Yet, the Trinity Schools had a proven track record (which I had seen myself in the lives of my two nephews) in encouraging a culture marked by "the discovery of truth, the practice of goodness, the creation of beauty, the development of intellectual and aesthetic habits of the mind, and cultivation of servant leadership" and committed to "the wise care and governance of

His creation and in the building of His kingdom." This was their mission, and it accurately described the "why" of our Upper School as well.

Our teachers embraced this new Upper School gloss on our unchanging mission and settled into adapting the Trinity Curriculum to our existing one, with the goal of making the transition from Grades 8 to 9 supported and predictable. Our "why" involved practical work—revising our math curriculum, moving books from one year to another (*Tale of Two Cities*, a Grade 8 read, now moved to Grade Ten), retrofitting eighth-grade Latin so ninth-grade Latin students would be ready to grapple with Cicero, Caesar, and even Virgil. Middle School students learned that their accelerated math option placed them on the path to Multivariable Calculus in their Senior year.

Still, in speaking about the key role of teachers in The Wilberforce Upper School, for someone to attribute the school's success to how our instructors adapted curriculum, parlayed skills, or revealed field expertise missed our essence. What made, and still makes, The Wilberforce Upper School distinct from other local high schools is our teachers' focused investment in students' spiritual and character growth. Even while Wilberforce teachers lead their students toward academic and intellectual maturity, they care for their students' hearts and souls. Concurrent to their providing a rich feast of skills and truths, Wilberforce teachers model their faith and exemplify life choices and habits that engender strong churches, strong families, and strong neighborhoods.

High school's rhetoric years are a formative time, as students reflect upon and expand the facts and rules that they have learned in the grammar and logic years. At a time when students are tempted to curate their activities and opportunities for the college admission officers, we remind them that our school interests lie not merely in four finite years, but on what Simon Sinek calls "the infinite game": a life lived to serve others and to transform our world.

So, as we at Wilberforce chose to embrace texts like *The Social Contract*, *Dante's Inferno*, and *The Brothers Karamazov*, we also made a more difficult decision to forgo AP tests. Our choices meant our teachers called their students to submit the sometimes uproar of the high school years to the wisdom of the ages, to prepare for independent adulthood by laboring together in a community of learners led by adults who called their students "to come up higher." As we emphasized discussion and writing (Humane Letters) and research-discovery (STEM classes) over "teach and tell" methodology, Wilberforce created a very different high school experience.

Let me illustrate one practical implication of the "why" of The Wilberforce Upper School. Our choosing to view technology as a tool and not a teacher led us to severely restrict cell phone usage during the school day. This "why-based" choice has proven wise. Because students are not spending their time face down, looking at their cell phones, or even face forward, looking at their computers, they discover a culture of conversation. They learn to interact with each other with the empathy that comes from serious listening; they learn to be more humane.

Always more of a process school (with the focus on whom we are forming) than a product school (with the focus on which colleges admit our students), our methods are as different as our outcomes. Whether the class is Biology, Bible, or European History and Letters, teacher and student choose to put themselves under the text, to prefer primary texts and first-hand experience to secondary and second-hand learning, to hear different (and often contradictory) voices, and to wrestle with truth with the end that study proves civil, humane, and transformative. To do this, teachers are both mentors and coaches, teaching their students to embrace the Great Conversation with energy, humility, and wonder.

So what does this education mean for Wilberforce Upper School students? As I write this, we have graduated five classes, with yet another readied to leave in a few months. Word back from alumni says that we are achieving our goals. Let me quote from a recent email from one of our earliest graduates, in which she explains why she joined her college's debating society and how her Wilberforce perspectives continue to inform her activities and even her career:

Well into freshman year with all my calculus and chemistry courses, I realized how much I missed HL [our abbreviation for our Humane Letters courses]; I could not pass up the opportunity to talk about Dante and Plato again . . .! Moving slowly in the direction of environmental education and climate advocacy . . . my next steps after undergrad will look . . . somewhere near the intersection of nature, writing, and people.

How these Wilberforce students use their foundational intellectual skills and qualities of mind and heart varies greatly, but we aspire to prepare each one for a life well-lived, a life that serves their fellows and pleases their Creator. We will look more at this "how" in the next two chapters.

The How: Sharing
a Curriculum in Community

In the last chapter, we began to think about the teachers
and texts that have enabled Wilberforce Upper School
students to achieve both a depth of inquiry and a sense of
wonder in their learning, as well as to ignite their passion
and perseverance in serving God and neighbor. How do
you take a diverse group of girls and boys—including some
whose first language is not English and many whose outside school interests include sports, part-time jobs, coding,
dance, service, social media, and body-building (in other
words, normal teens)—and turn them into a community
that wrestles graciously and profoundly with the issues of
government and politics, ethics and law, justice and lifestyle,
science and faith? For us, the answer to that question revolves
around our teaching method: discussion and inquiry-based
study focused upon a set of shared "living texts," as Charlotte
Mason would say.

Using these texts, Wilberforce students work to understand and evaluate arguments, trace the effects of diverse
opinions on history and culture, reproduce and/or analyze
important laboratory and programming feats, produce and
perform beautiful music, theater, and art. They expand their
knowledge base as they learn to analyze, critique, correlate,

and apply that knowledge. Surprisingly, behind these accomplishments lies the controversial fact that the Wilberforce students study the same curricula. For many in the twenty-first century, a shared high school curriculum is a radical (and suspect) idea.

To begin, I should clarify what I mean when I speak of the Upper School's shared curricula. This means that all students take four years of Humane Letters (a history-language arts combination), four years of math, four years of science, four years of language (one ancient and three modern), four years of art, two of music, two of drama, and four years of Scripture studies. The only possible electives appear in modern language (the choice of Spanish or Mandarin), mathematics (two different speeds for the first three years of similar courses and, in the fourth year, a choice between Statistics and Multivariable Calculus), and, finally, a fourth-year science alternative (either Physics 2 or Biochemistry). Stated another way, all Wilberforce Upper School students study Algebra, Pre-Calculus, Geometry, and Calculus. All read the same literature books and primary source history. All students participate in two plays, learn drawing and painting, and sing in a chorus. All study Biology, Chemistry, and Physics. All learn to write analytically, recite orally, discuss civilly, program effectively, and compute accurately.

What are the outcomes of such carefully chosen shared texts and activities? The first is that our students are not "fixed mindset" specialists. At Wilberforce, we celebrate "a growth mindset," what researcher Carol Dweck defines as the belief that one's "most basic abilities can be developed through dedication and hard work—brains and talent are just the starting point. This view creates a love of learning and a resilience that is essential for great accomplishment" (2015). Repeatedly, students have entered our Upper School from other institutions, professing that they "could not write" or "were not 'math people'," and then later concluded that they loved writing or they wanted a math-heavy career. We believe that high school is too young an age to close doors to fields of study or career options. We want our students to uncover a broad array of knowledge through which to interpret their lives and plan for their future endeavors. In a current cultural environment where the average worker changes careers from three to seven times in a lifetime, such a broad exposure seems not only wise but also advised.

Beyond preparing students for a changing future, what is the present value of the Upper School shared curriculum? A shared curriculum builds community. It provides an equal foundation from which students can discuss new material, new ideas, and new events. It allows teachers to allude to a collective body of knowledge and expands their ability to connect the dots for their students. A shared curriculum provides both identity and confidence. Wilberforce Upper School students know that their education has prepared them well for today and for tomorrow.

Understanding that Wilberforce has a shared curriculum is not as important as understanding what that shared curriculum is. This shared curriculum is not a straitjacket, a blacklist, a constraint, nor a particular and limited view of the world. Instead, our curriculum is a jumping-off point for creativity, understanding, and application. Even with their shared studies, Wilberforce Upper School students have many opportunities to branch out and explore personal areas of interest. Most times, student paper topics are self-chosen and reflect personal concerns. In math class, where one financial project involves mortgages and budgets, some students opt to finance a six-million-dollar mansion while others choose a mobile home. Other examples abound. Old Testament Proverbs projects have included script-writing, video lessons, art depictions of minor prophets, and even complex origami. Spanish class celebrations involve singing popular songs, profiling a variety of Spanish artists, and making cookbooks and menus complete with samples of authentic cuisines.

Even regarding art class imitations (a supposedly creativity-limiting teaching method), student works reveal great variety. For example, when tenth-grade students study Georgia O'Keefe's vibrant colors and powerful images, each student picks personal subject matter to depict with "O'Keefe-ian" detail. By twelfth grade, students choose both their media and their reference material. Their senior portraits and projects prove capstone pieces of beauty and individuality.

Perhaps the most prominent area where students elect their own focus of study occurs with their Project Week activities. Every year during the first week of January, Wilberforce Upper School students stay away from school and work on individual projects. These projects include chemistry experiments in Grade 10 and service projects in Grade 12. Ninth-graders write long research papers on areas of American life that interest them. Over the years, these papers have dealt with politics (such as the role of Progressivism in the US), with the military (including weapon development), and with culture (from the development of the Model T to the theft of the Star of India sapphire). No matter the topic, these ninth-graders experience the thrill of deep work and original research.

In their junior year, students travel one step further and create what we term a "passion" project. In this project, each works with his or her chosen faculty advisor to explore in depth an area of interest. In addition to preparing their projects—which range from a children's book to a diabolical ballad, a series of portraits to a marketable product, from an artificial arm to a bird migration study, students complete this passion exploration process by defending their work orally before a three-person panel and many invited guests.

Students see these Junior Projects as a culmination of their work in the first three years of high school. The common curriculum has equipped them with speaking, writing, artistic, and computer skills, as well as with leveraging their mentoring relationships with teachers. While the principal purpose of these projects is to allow students to explore and wonder at a deep level, we have also found some helpful byproducts. For example, students learn how to explain their work orally and face hard questions with ease. Students are able to try out areas of future interest. Even more, they now have something specific to write about in college applications or to share in their interviews. Of course, occasionally a student is even knighted, as one of our students was, in appreciation for her passion project, an illustrated book on Hungary before and after Communism.

I hope that by now requiring a shared curriculum does not sound quite as Draconian as it might have when my readers first heard it mentioned. In fact, at our school, non-humanities Upper School teachers often elect to read one of our HL books during their summer "down time" or to sing alongside the student chorus for our Fine Arts Week. In other words, our teachers are a little jealous of their students; the faculty realizes they missed out on a lot during their own high school education. Maybe, after reading this chapter, you feel that way as well.

The What: A Lifelong Learning Community

The four years of high school pass quickly. Courses and halls that looked daunting to the new ninth-grader seem tame to the second-semester senior. When our Upper School students leave Wilberforce, they possess an array of knowledge. But amassing storehouses of knowledge (even knowledge that is classically good, true, and beautiful) is not our school's main goal. We know that long after thermodynamics and Sophocles are distant memories, our former students will remember—and interact with—the friends and mentors with whom they shared life during their Upper School years. By discussing and arguing, running and performing alongside each other, planning family nights for the Lower School, and filming silly morning messages, their educational experience grows stronger, deeper, and richer. From such genuine community, kingdom transformation flows.

Because students are not mere "brains on a stick," the Wilberforce Upper School is designed to incorporate hearts and emotions, drives and passions, connections and experiences. Stated another way, we at Wilberforce focus more on relationship-building than on SAT scores and current GPAs. Of course, scores and GPAs are important, just not primary. When students belong to a robust and lively learning community, how they treat their fellow students is more critical than numbers alone. In a small school, the student you argue with during HL class may well be your goalie in the afternoon's lacrosse game, your prompter for the play you are rehearsing in fourth period, and the House leader you partner with to encourage Grade Six students to sign up for the knock-out (basketball) tournament.

Whether engaging in curricular or co-curricular activities, our Upper School students develop the essential life skills of collaboration and co-elevation, as they discover together how to live out our school's mission. And it is not only in classes that students test another's ideas, try out theories, act out interpretations, create laboratories, and evaluate mathematical modeling. During their co-curriculars, students also build their relational muscles. In class, they may debate Lincoln and Douglas's opinions; outside of class, they use parliamentary debate against peers all across the country. In chorus, students prepare a few beautiful songs each semester; outside of class, they create a yearly musical and form a cappella groups and chamber orchestras (and sometimes even write and perform their own musical). In theater, they prepare and present two curricular plays; at other times, students perform skits and radio shows, make videos and podcasts, and climax each year with their variety show called "Symposium." After-school hours allow time as well for strength training and interscholastic sports, with guys and girls not only competing each season but also assuming team leadership roles.

At this point, you may be asking yourself, how is what is being described different from what occurs in other high schools—don't all these schools offer performances (music and drama) and sports competitions? The answer echoes the concept of a "growth mindset" that we discussed in Appendix Chapter 3. At our Upper School, students are free to "do it all"; they are not forced to choose between being a "theater person" and a "sports person." We want high school to be a time for experimentation and discovery, for moving outside one's "comfort zone" and into new cohorts and experiences.

It takes sacrifice to create this celebration of options. While most school teams practice five, or even six, days a week, our teams practice only four (making our recent top showing in our division's cross country competitions that much more amazing). Our sport teams' meeting only four days a week leaves one afternoon open for students to pursue the arts—such as drama, chamber music, debate, or drawing. In addition to availing themselves of these "Arts Tuesdays," our students are encouraged to make good use of a special period (called "Consultation") that occurs in the middle of each school day. While students may use Consultation as a study hall or to take advantage of faculty office hours, this period is also a time for a cappella rehearsals, student publications creation, and other student-initiated clubs. At Wilberforce, we make it easy for students to explore and risk. Perhaps this emphasis on options is one reason why in 2019 our school was voted the "top arts school" in New Jersey.

Before I leave the topic of community building, I must describe the key co-curricular that binds Wilberforce students together: our House System. In a small school with a common curriculum, students at the same grade level find natural fodder for bonding. Sharing courses and assignments, individual Wilberforce classes often gain unique identities as they share life together. But to bind people across multiple class levels is harder. The Wilberforce House System addresses this multiple-grade concern, linking all seven classes of our Middle and Upper Schools.

Our Wilberforce Middle/Upper School has four Houses. Named after members of the famed Clapham Community (men and women who worked with William Wilberforce to battle slavery and injustice), our four houses are: Macauley, Venn, Thornton, and More. Each house contains a relatively equal number of students from Grades 6 through 12, along with an equal number of faculty advisors. Houses form a team—celebrated with house colors, flags, mascots, mottos, shields, and swag. In recent years, the *Harry Potter* books have made the idea of "houses" more or less understandable to Americans. While lacking a sorting hat and other exciting paraphernalia, Wilberforce's Houses each construct their own identities. To help with this process, each September the entire Middle and Upper Schools participate in a two-day retreat and tournament. Here, with appropriate fanfare, each House initiates its new members and then quickly enfolds them into the ongoing competition for glory (and trophy).

These Wilberforce Houses are primarily student-led. While one or two teachers serve as the schoolwide "House Governors" and sounding board for student leadership, each house has four officers (with the positions of President, Build, Serve, and Tournament) who manage the various dimensions of House Life. Even if the overseeing role of President is probably obvious, the other three jobs deserve further explanation. The Build officer organizes social events to bring students together, such as game and movie nights, House lunches and outings (examples include hikes or ice skating). The Serve officer points the House outward, leading the members in sharing Christ, alleviating needs, and spreading encouragement. While service projects are as diverse as the students that do them, over the years, House members have cleaned up parks and churches, raked to raise money for service trips, written letters to soldiers and prisoners, fed patrons at rescue missions, and packed Christmas presents for needy children. Last, and deeply appreciated, stands the Tournament officer who helps to plan and run inter-House competitions. These contests range from Spike-ball eliminations to spelling bees, from best limericks to best trick shots, from photographic art to sumo wrestling (a feat that students accomplish while wearing inflatable body suits).

Throughout the year, the House Governor maintains the ongoing and frequently publicized competition standings. In May, the winning House receives much praise, along with the consummate honor of having its House shield hung highest in the student MPR, the room where lunchtime occurs daily.

This placement means that House members are regularly reminded both of past triumphs and of their current quest to elevate both their scores and their shield's placement.

As House members, students learn sportsmanship (another source for House points during hard-fought tournaments) and accountability, personal responsibility and group dynamics. Still, if you asked a Wilberforce student to describe the benefits of the House System, their answers would be much simpler—the chance to know students from other classes, the opportunities to strategize to create a win, and, most of all, the fun, the laughter, and the memories.

Music groups and sports teams, House competitions and debate tournaments—Wilberforce Upper School offers students ways to investigate and experiment, learn and laugh, and to bring deeper levels of community back into the classroom. Adding an Upper School to The Wilberforce JK-8 School has proved a wonderful completion of the adventure begun in Explorers One. It has affirmed and extended all that the founders hoped when they began dreaming about a classical Christian school in Princeton, New Jersey. The Wilberforce Upper School mission is big, bold, and optimistic. In and out of the classroom, we train student minds and hearts to rigorously explore reality, to cultivate lifelong habits and loves, and to be servants in, and builders of, God's kingdom.

About The Wilberforce School

The founders of The Wilberforce School (TWS) sought to establish a school in Princeton that would be both Christ-exalting and academically excellent. Founded in 2005, the school's mission is to provide a distinctly Christian education characterized by academic excellence and joyful discovery within a classical framework.

Our understanding of God as Creator and of his saving purposes in Jesus Christ underlies all of our teaching and conduct. Thus we place special emphasis on honoring the Lordship of Jesus Christ over all things, teaching from a biblical view of the world, applying biblical truth to all of life so that the hearts and minds of our students might know, love, and obey God, and pursuing excellence so that everything we do is an act of worship.

We strive to nurture young people who have a genuine love of learning, who are equipped to live as vibrant Christians in their various callings, and who can articulate and defend the Christian message with clarity, creativity, and conviction.

Our school is named after William Wilberforce because he lived out the combination that we seek to instill in our students: Wilberforce united his classical training—in particular, his skills in rhetoric—with his devotion to Christ and applied his talents and passions to the great issues of his day, most notably the abolition of the British slave trade.

TWS is classical in its embrace of the trivium, its emphasis on the classics, and its study of Latin. Our view of the way children learn is also influenced by the ideas of Charlotte Mason, a nineteenth- and twentieth-century British educator who pioneered methods that took advantage of a child's natural curiosity and delight in discovery and emphasized the formation of godly habits as the basis for a lifetime of academic and spiritual vitality.

Our overarching desire is to see God at work in our school as he draws our students' hearts to love Christ and shapes their minds to be active, vigorous, and informed by biblical truth.

TWS serves students in grades Junior K through 12. To learn more about The Wilberforce School, please visit www.wilberforceschool.org.

CPSIA information can be obtained
at www.ICGtesting.com
Printed in the USA
BVHW041218020621
608663BV00001B/1